UN
STUCK

Overcoming the
Thresholds that Limit Us

CRYSTAL M. NEUBAUER

Details in some of the stories and anecdotes have been changed to protect the identities of the persons involved. Unless otherwise indicated, all Scripture quotations are taken from the Holy Bible, New Living Translation, copyright © 1996, 2004, 2015 by Tyndale House Foundation. Used by permission of Tyndale House Publishers, a Division of Tyndale House Ministries, Carol Stream, Illinois 60188. All rights reserved. Scripture taken from the Holy Bible, New King James Version®, copyright © 1982 by Thomas Nelson. Used by permission. All rights reserved. Scripture taken from the Holy Bible, New international Version®, copyright © 1984. Grand Rapids: Zondervan Publishing House. All Greek and Hebrew word studies are from www.biblehub.com. 2020.

The synonyms for "brought to light" are from www.collinsdictionary.com. 2020.

Wakeman, Cy. (2010). Reality-Based Leadership. (1st edition). Jossey-Bass: San Francisco, CA.

Copyright © 2020 by Crystal Neubauer.

All rights reserved. This book or any portion thereof may not be reproduced or used in any manner whatsoever without the express written permission of the publisher except for the use of brief quotations in a book review.

Photography by Josh Eklund Photography

Publishing Services provided by Paper Raven Books
Printed in the United States of America
First Printing, 2020

Paperback ISBN= 978-1-7357458-0-0
Hardback ISBN= 978-1-7357458-1-7

TABLE OF CONTENTS

Introduction	1
Part One: We're Stuck	3
Chapter 1: We All Get Stuck Sometimes	5
Chapter 2: We Each Have a Threshold	17
Part Two: Why We Get and Stay Stuck	37
Chapter 3: Our Threshold Is in Our Thinking	39
Chapter 4: The Nature of Truth	51
Chapter 5: The Nature of a Lie	69
Chapter 6: How We Get Trapped in Our Thoughts	97
Chapter 7: Getting Unstuck Is a Process	117
Chapter 8: Determine Your Commitment	125
Chapter 9: Find the Truth	157
Chapter 10: Act with Courage	185
Chapter 11: Trust the Process	209
Chapter 12: It's Not Just About You	221
Acknowledgements	225

INTRODUCTION

In my 20 years of public speaking, ministry, and training experience, I have never found a message that resonates more than that of "getting unstuck." I've never taught a principle that more positively impacted lives in a long-term way than the Threshold Model I will introduce in this book. Throughout the ages, people have gotten stuck, so this is nothing new. However, we have more information and resources at our fingertips today than ever before—and yet the problem remains. My goal in writing this book isn't to deliver more information, but to introduce you to powerful principles that can transform the way you think, feel, and live.

This is my story of how my faith helped me get unstuck. It's raw, and it's real, but I knew it needed to be to reach the right audience. I've had people ask me why I didn't write this as a secular book, with the thought that it might have broader appeal. Trust me, I thought about it. In the end, I realized Jesus is the most vital part of the unstuck equation. Information and self-help books are great (that's why I'm writing this one!) but are marginally effective alone. Leaving Jesus out would leave my story unfinished. Even more so, it would be an injustice to the reader who needs hope for their own story.

If you don't believe Jesus is the Son of God, or you don't know what to think about Him, I want to encourage you to read this book with an open mind. The fact that you are reading a book on how to get unstuck tells me you know, deep down, you are missing something, someone. That someone is Jesus. I hope that you read this book, and your life is radically changed, not because they are my words or my experiences, but because you've seen a clear picture of what Jesus can and will do in your life.

Getting unstuck is hard work, so I've attempted to make it as practical and straightforward as possible. This is in no way to give you the impression that I have the secret formula and am forever immune from getting stuck in my own life. I'm still learning these things—in fact, I've learned a great deal in the process of writing this book. My goal is to take what I've learned, organize and articulate it in a way that makes sense, and then share it with the hope that it brings the same freedom to you that it did to me. I see this book as a guide to walk you through a process. In addition to sharing the concepts behind how I got unstuck in my own life, I've also included relatable stories, along with activities, prayer starters, and reflection questions throughout to help you along the way. Additional tools and resources can be found at www.nowgrowingforward.com.

PART ONE

We're Stuck

CHAPTER 1

WE ALL GET STUCK SOMETIMES

It happens to me every summer. My family owns farmland with a small lake and a couple of cabins. In the spring, summer, and fall months, you will often find me there, enjoying the peace on the weekends. The area is several acres, so the entire family pitches in to keep up the property. One of my primary jobs is mowing, which involves operating a commercial-sized orange zero-turn mower. The task takes about 90 minutes each week throughout the summer, but I pop in my earbuds, put on my favorite podcast, and drive the zero-turn mower as though I stole it. I've been told I drive it like a race car, and I consider that to be a compliment!

Zero-turn mowers require a different skill set than a mower with a typical steering wheel, so though they aren't hard to drive, there is a bit of a learning curve. The first time I drove ours, I ran into a tree, and I'm sure I looked like quite the fool! I'm a seasoned driver now, and I've learned the nuances of maneuvering around objects at breakneck speed.

Most of the mowing is on high ground, so my primary focus is seeing how straight I can make my lines and still drive it fast like a race car. It takes more effort than you might think to accomplish both at the same time. After mowing the lawn around the cabins, I mow a walking path that encircles the entire lake. From above, the lake looks more like a hand with fingers, and the whole path is nearly a mile because of the way the lake juts out. The route follows the shape of the lake, and in some areas, it runs right next to the shoreline. It is inevitable that at least once a year while mowing the path along the edge of the lake, I come across a spot where the ground appears to be dry but is instead soft from recent rain. The soft ground gives way under the mower, and before I know it, I'm stuck. It happens every summer.

Though this lawnmower illustration is a simple one, it carries some powerful principles that apply to our lives and will serve as foundational truths for the remainder of this book. If you've ever gotten your car stuck, you know how frustrating it can be when you can't make progress, no matter how hard you try. This same frustration exists when we become "stuck" in our lives. When you are stuck, you feel powerless, frustrated, and even hopeless.

There's no shame in being stuck, but it's tempting to beat ourselves up—that's what the enemy of your soul, Satan, wants you to do. He heaps shame and discouragement on you, hoping you'll dig yourself deeper. He wants you to believe you are stuck because there is something wrong with you or because you are a failure. Ironically, my dad often admonishes me to "not get stuck," and yet I do. I know better, but it still happens. Every time I end up stuck, I call my dad for help, and he never shames me. He usually just chuckles and then lets me know he'll be there shortly to help me. In a lot of ways, my dad is like my Heavenly Father because He never shames me for getting stuck, either!

Chapter 1: We All Get Stuck Sometimes

I'm a pro at driving the lawnmower, and I've mowed that particular path countless times. I could almost do it with my eyes closed. I recognize the difference between dry ground and wet ground, and yet I still end up stuck. Not because I'm incompetent or inept, but because it's the nature of the process of mowing. The appearance of the dry surface deceives me into believing it's also dry under the surface. It is my belief system that fails me.

This principle is true for each one of us. We don't get stuck because we set out to do so. We don't get stuck because we're bad people, are unintelligent, or because we lack a desire to live a purposeful life. No, we get stuck because it's part of the natural process of living in a fallen and deceptive world. More specifically, we get stuck because we begin to believe things that aren't true about ourselves, our circumstances, and God.

Many people long to live a more fulfilling, purposeful life, but they don't know how to get there. Others have previously lived with great purpose, passion, and vision, but have become lukewarm over time. Others believe they have messed up their lives to such a degree that they deserve to be miserable, while still others feel so worn down and defeated by their circumstances that it's hard to envision a different life. If you fall into any of these categories, don't allow shame to paralyze you from making changes. There's no shame in being stuck. Instead of thinking of your current state as permanent, think of it as a starting point for whatever comes next.

It's important to note that getting stuck is a process. The process of getting stuck with the lawnmower begins long before I recognize I'm stuck. It's not until my progress comes to a sudden halt that I realize I'm getting stuck. In our lives, it's also a gradual process that happens over time. It's never one thing that gets us stuck but instead a culmination of both subconscious and conscious beliefs and the corresponding decisions that follow. We often don't realize we are getting stuck until it's too late.

One of the sneakiest characteristics of being stuck is that we often don't recognize it early on. A couple of years ago, I began feeling very restless and dissatisfied with my life. It wasn't that my life was terrible—I had a great family, a great church, and a thriving career. I was genuinely thankful for these things and knew I had a life many would envy. But under the surface, I knew I was living far below my potential and calling. I was turning a blind eye to my dysfunctions so I could maintain unhealthy relationships. I had issues of the heart I was hiding while giving the impression that I was entirely right with God. I had unresolved wounds buried beneath layers of my religion. Because of this, I began to feel stuck in my relationships, ministry, and career. I didn't realize it at the time, but my discontentment wasn't with others. My displeasure was with myself. I resented myself for living below my potential, and I used that resentment to perpetuate the very things in my life that were causing me to stay stuck. It's astonishing how often we perpetuate our misery.

One day, I woke up and decided I was tired of living below my created potential. It was the Holy Spirit using my growing dissatisfaction as an invitation to be transformed, and a launching point for what He wanted to orchestrate in my life. In that moment of surrender, I became ready to do whatever it took to get unstuck. I didn't know what that looked like or where to start; I just knew I didn't want to keep living in the same way. I was tired of feeling stuck.

When I look back on it now, I realize my restlessness was the work of the Holy Spirit, stirring in me a hunger for something more. Just like hunger prompts us to go to the kitchen to prepare a meal, this kind of desire inspires us to change ourselves. Until

I wanted something more, I wasn't ready for the hard work of repentance, surrender, and courageous obedience. It started with fierce honesty with myself and with the Lord, admitting I was stuck and couldn't dig myself out on my own.

That admission was humbling for me. As a natural leader, I'm used to making things happen. I'm known for initiating change, breaking the status quo, and leading projects to completion. I help people and projects get unstuck. It's what I naturally do. And yet here I was, stuck because of my own doing. It was humbling, but at the same time, it was freeing because that admission permitted me to dream again. It enabled me to want more. It allowed me to become more. I didn't know it then, but that admission was the beginning of an unbelievably painful and rewarding life-changing journey. Admitting I was stuck was the beginning of getting unstuck.

Getting unstuck is also a process. Just as it is a process to get the lawnmower stuck, it is often a more prolonged and messier process to get it unstuck. In my own life, I didn't get unstuck overnight. It was a culmination of many decisions to surrender to Jesus, many small acts of courage, and many raw conversations with others that helped me get unstuck. We'll spend a great deal of time expounding on the process of getting unstuck throughout this book, but it's essential to know that God knew His people would get stuck. He's not surprised by it, nor is He unprepared for it. He is certainly not daunted by it. If you consider the entirety of the Word, it's the overarching story of His people getting stuck, and God providing a way out and forward. He delights in leading His people out of the places where they feel stuck. It is the essence of salvation, faith, and all spiritual growth.

We cannot have authentic conversations about discipleship without embracing the realities of how we become stuck and unstuck. Paul speaks to this discipleship process in Philippians 2:12, "*Work hard to show the results of your salvation, obeying God with deep reverence and fear.*" Getting unstuck is the difficult, but rewarding, process of working the results of salvation into our thoughts, emotions, behaviors, and every crevice of our lives. When you make homemade bread, you work the yeast mixture into the flour to activate the gluten. It is the process of kneading that gives it texture and strength and allows the yeast to be activated. Likewise, it is the process of getting unstuck that strengthens us and triggers the realities of salvation in all aspects of our lives. Jesus isn't just interested in activating initial salvation where our eternity in heaven is secured. He longs to bring the freedom of the cross into every aspect of your life!

If you are stuck, it means there is a dead place in your life that Jesus longs to resurrect. I love how Paul says it in Ephesians 1:19–20, "*I also pray that you will understand the incredible greatness of God's power for us who believe him. This is the same mighty power that raised Christ from the dead and seated him in the place of honor at God's right hand in the heavenly realms.*" The Greek word for power is *dunamis*, which can be translated as mighty works or wonderful works and is the origin of our English words *dynamic* and *dynamite*. This power is capable of doing so much in and through you that it will inspire a sense of wonder in others. In other words, when *dunamis* power is at work in your life, others will see it and be in awe!

It is this explosive power of the cross that brings life where there is death. If you study many of the instances where the New Testament uses *dunamis*, you will often find it describing how power transforms a situation or condition—people changed from death to life, from sickness to health, and from bondage into freedom. That same power is actively transforming you from death to life, sickness to wholeness, bound to free, and from stuck to unstuck!

Without the cross, being stuck would be the permanent state of our lives. But with the cross, we have the power to overcome anything that conspires to keep us from experiencing life to the fullest. We are to be OVER-comers, not barely-comers. We are to be MORE than conquerors, not barely-conquerors.

Many of us have bought into the lie that the Christian life is mundane and that we should accept the status quo as the norm. But, how can a person's life, alive with the results of salvation, be mundane? There is nothing ordinary about what Jesus did for us on the cross! The intention of the cross is not just to help us "get by" but instead to give us access to all that God has for us. Living in survival mode robs us of the power of the cross. It makes the cross a mere placebo that carries the promise of *dunamis* power, without the realities of that power revealed in our lives. Said another way, we like the thought of *dunamis* power, but not as much as we enjoy the comfort and convenience of mundane life. Believers have access to that power, but we must be brave enough to welcome its activity in our lives. After all, not every dead bone wants to come back to life, not every heart wants to be made whole, and not every stuck person wants to get unstuck.

Let's be clear about what's at stake when we remain stuck. There is a real enemy of your soul who wants you to not only get stuck but to stay stuck. He wants you to live below your potential. He wants discouragement to hang over your head like a black cloud, following you wherever you go. He wants you to live a life of abbreviated purpose, stunted growth, and "just getting by." Keeping you stuck is part of his strategy.

There is also a very real Champion of your soul who eagerly wants you to get unstuck so you can walk in His freedom, favor, and blessing for your life. He has more for you than the life you are currently living. No matter how much you have accomplished or become, or no matter how much you have failed, He has more for you. With Jesus, there is always more.

Being stuck is a universal human condition, so you're not alone. It shows no favoritism, is not partial to any age, generation, or race, and affects believers and non-believers alike. I've accepted that it's an inevitable part of life, but I'm also putting my faith in the fact that staying stuck doesn't have to be inevitable. Because of the cross, we live according to different rules. Remaining stuck is not our destiny, it's not our purpose, and it's not our identity! Jesus has so much more for you and me.

My prayer is this book will stir anticipation in your hearts and spirits for what comes next. Jesus's story for your life never ends with being stuck. In the same way that His story didn't end when He took His last breath on the cross, your story isn't over. I believe there's something in you that Jesus longs to resurrect. He has so much more for you. My hope is that you will come to that same conclusion, and as you do, you will become filled with new hope, fresh vision, and a renewed passion for life.

Take heart, my friend, your season of being stuck is coming to an end. His love and power are on the scene and actively working to transform you. He is fully able, more than enough, and entirely willing to lead you forward. You're about to step into what God has next for you.

Activity: How do I know if I'm stuck?

Many people are stuck but haven't recognized it or had the words to label it. It can be challenging to define what it means to be stuck, and it looks a little different for everyone. One of the ways to identify if you are stuck is to envision what life looks like when you aren't stuck. If that vision isn't your reality, you are stuck. Here are six powerful questions to help you get started.

1. If my life were living up to my potential, how might my life be different?

_____
_____
_____
_____

2. If my relationships were healthier, how might my life be different?

_____
_____
_____
_____

3. If I were free from unresolved hurt from my past, how might my life be different?

_____
_____
_____
_____

4. If I thought about myself the way God thinks about me, how might my life be different?

_____
_____
_____
_____

5. If I felt complete freedom to be myself, how might my life be different?

_____
_____
_____
_____

6. If I could change a habit or conquer an addiction, how might my life be different?

_____
_____
_____
_____

If your answer to any of those questions is something different than your current life, you are stuck.

We all need help sometimes.

Once my mower is stuck, the only way to get it out is to get a chain and pull it out with another vehicle, like my Jeep Wrangler. One person drives the Jeep, the other operates the mower, and both move forward at the same time. The extra power of the Jeep allows the mower to overcome the force of being stuck. It's a far stretch to compare my Jeep to the Holy Spirit (although I'm pretty sure they are both gifts from heaven), but in reality, that's what the Holy Spirit does for us. He provides the extra power, strategy, and strength we need to get unstuck. He helps us do what we cannot do on our own.

Whoever sits on the mower must partner with the one who is supplying the power and the strategy. In the same way, we partner with the Holy Spirit to get unstuck. Our role is not passive but one of actively submitting, vigorously seeking His direction, and courageously responding with obedience. I can assure you your willingness and cooperation are critical. We can't get unstuck by doing things our way and in our power. That is what gets us stuck in the first place!

Our desire for self-sufficiency keeps us from asking for the help we need. Instead, we sit and spin our wheels and often in the opposite direction of what God wants. I can't tell you how many times I've remained stuck because I wanted to do things my way and refused to surrender to the process He's doing in me. My resistance creates activity in my life but not progress. We mistake spinning wheels for progress when, in reality, our efforts toward self-sufficiency usually dig us deeper into our ruts.

The opposite of self-sufficiency is surrender. This is the place where we invite Him into our need and submit to His strength and wisdom. As we rely on Him, He encourages us and surrounds us with others who can provide support. We have a dual need for both God and others. If you want to get unstuck, now is an excellent time to get used to that idea. It will be crucial to your journey. To reject our need for either God or others is to deny our very design. You can't get unstuck on your own. To keep you from this vital encouragement and support, Satan will do everything he can to convince you that you are all alone in your stuck state. He wants you to believe no one else understands, and no one else cares. Based on countless conversations I've had with those who have been stuck and are in the process of getting unstuck, I can assure you that you are not alone. You're joining a movement of people who are tired of going through the motions and going around the mountain.

This book will provide valuable information, ideas, and resources to help lead you through the process, but this is only a start. For some, this may mark the beginning of a transformative relationship with God. For those of you who already have a relationship, now is the time to double down. He has to become your top priority, or you will end up doing it all from your strength and your way. If you cry out to Him for help, you will experience His power in ways you never have before, for His strength is made perfect in our weakness. If you commit yourself to His process, you're about to see significant breakthroughs and experience profound, long-lasting transformation. It will be well worth it.

Before you read any further, take a moment and invite Jesus into the area you are stuck. He's ready and willing to partner with you to help you get unstuck. Here's a prayer to get you started:

PRAYER POINT: *Jesus, I am stuck. I've tried to get unstuck on my own, and I can't do it. Your Word promises that You are attentive to those who recognize their need for You, and right now, I confess I need You. I acknowledge You died on the cross, forgiving me from my sins so I could be made new and whole. In You, it is possible to become free from the things that entangle me and keep me stuck. I invite You to speak to me as I read this book, illuminate the things I need to see, stir the areas in my heart that need stirring, and give me clarity for how to move forward. I am weak, and I need Your strength. In Jesus's name, Amen.*

Your prayer just now didn't fall on deaf ears. 1 John 5:14–15 says, *"And we are confident that he hears us whenever we ask for anything that pleases him. And since we know he hears us when we make our requests, we also know that he will give us what we ask for."* You can rest assured He's pleased by your prayer and help is on the way.

CHAPTER 2
WE EACH HAVE A THRESHOLD

The Threshold Model

As a visual learner, I understand concepts best when I can see them. The Lord often speaks to me in visuals to help me understand the relationship between ideas and how He works in our lives. He showed me the Threshold Model to teach me how we get stuck and to illustrate the process of getting unstuck.

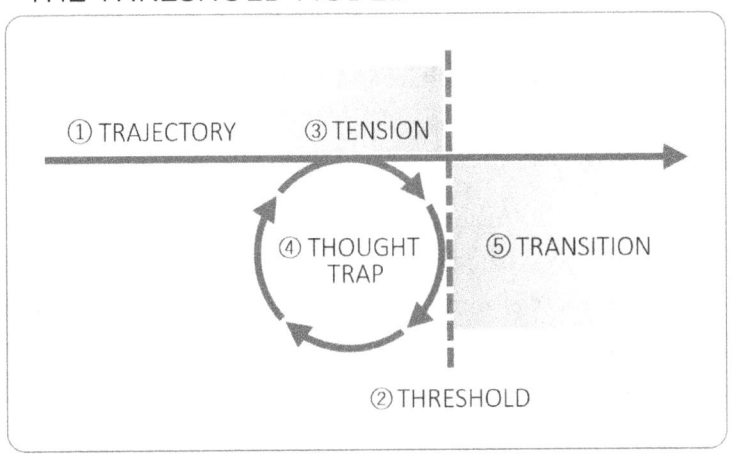

The central premise is that each one of us has a threshold that limits us. It is the reason we get and remain stuck. Understanding the various components of the model will help you identify the contributing factors in your life, as well as give you comprehensive knowledge of what to expect as you move through the process. Here is a brief description of each component, followed by more in-depth explanations:

1. **Trajectory** – The path, progression, and development of your life or an aspect of your life.
2. **Threshold** – What you must confront or cross over to grow to the next level. Said another way, it's the barrier or limiter that keeps you from transitioning into what God has for you next.
3. **Tension** – The place of struggle where you must decide whether you will seek to protect and maintain your current norm or if you will take a step of courage towards a new way of living.
4. **Thought Trap** – These traps are cyclical thinking resulting in cyclical behavior. Instead of breaking through our threshold, we often get stuck in these cycles.
5. **Transition** – The transition period is where you implement change. In this season, you learn how to think in new ways so you can learn to behave in new ways.

Your Trajectory

I was recently in Aruba. The island is beautiful and one of my favorites I've visited. But beyond the stunningly beautiful beaches and the well-cared-for tourist areas, there are hundreds of abandoned buildings, including hotels, waterparks, and businesses. Many of these buildings were left abruptly mid-

Chapter 2: We Each Have a Threshold

construction when the economy suffered. It's been years since construction began and ended on these buildings, so what remains are apocalyptic-looking structures. Some are simply frames, while others are nearly complete. Some have been boarded up, while others stand exposed to the elements and peering eyes. Each represents a blueprint full of promise that never fulfilled its potential. Each is a reminder of hopes and dreams that never came to fruition because of economic disruption.

This image is a sad depiction of many believers. The church is full of lukewarm believers who, in various states of being built by Christ, have abandoned the discipleship process because it got too hard, required too much, and meant giving up too much control. Believers who liked the idea of discipleship but were unwilling to cross the thresholds necessary to experience the rewards of discipleship. Believers who abandoned hopes and dreams because they seemed impossible. Or believers who wouldn't stay the course when discipleship disrupted their lives.

Our Designer meticulously created us packed full of potential, with layers of potential to be unveiled as we grow. I'm sure you've heard the term "reach your potential." I understand the intent behind this trendy phrase but believe our potential is not a far-off destination we are trying to reach. It is something that unfolds as we learn to trust God, and it is the evidence of progress.

The enemy doesn't initially target your potential, though that is his ultimate goal. Instead, he aims to keep you from progressing, for if he is successful with that, your potential is forfeited. He understands that our progress and potential are linked. One does not happen without the other. Unfortunately, many believers have sacrificed their potential because the work of progress was more than they bargained for.

We define a trajectory as the path or progression something is on. When you reference the model, the line with arrows represents your trajectory in life. It is the unfolding of your potential as you grow and progress. Simply put, it is your path of progress and growth. It may represent your life as a whole or could represent a specific aspect, such as a relationship, ministry, or career.

I've intentionally illustrated our trajectory as a horizontal line rather than the classic example of a trajectory where the path climbs upward. Here, we gain a realistic picture of what progress looks like within the Kingdom of God. It is God's will that you grow, progress, and experience success. And yet, how He defines and measures those things is significantly different than the world. The world says success is moving upward. The Kingdom says success is moving forward.

Unfortunately, moving forward doesn't always feel like moving forward. The process of emotional healing is a great example. There are many instances in my life when painful things I thought were resolved have suddenly resurfaced, causing me to feel like I've gone backward. Instead, I've discovered new layers of pain surfacing is a sign of progress and healing. Sometimes you have to go back to go forward.

Our trajectory isn't a straight, uninterrupted line. It rarely looks like what you think it will. For the sake of simplicity here, I've illustrated it as a straight line, but a more realistic representation would be ups, downs, and many thought loops and thresholds. We see a Biblical precedent for this. Every time Joseph took one step towards his destiny, something would happen to halt his forward progress. David was anointed king and then spent years in hiding in obscurity before stepping into the limelight. Moses had to flee to Midian after killing an Egyptian, which took him away from the very people he was to lead. Ultimately, God used these setbacks to accelerate their progress at the right time.

But if you took a snapshot of Joseph's life at various stages, you would label him a failure. While he sits in jail, his brothers prosper. If you took a snapshot of David hiding in a cave, you wouldn't call him a great king. If you only looked at Moses's time in Midian, you might label him a coward. But Joseph's humiliating moments prepared him for moments of honor down the road. David's hiding prepared him for the spotlight. Moses learned valuable lessons in Midian that allowed him to return to his people with the capacity and character needed to lead them out of slavery. Sometimes you have to fail to succeed, lose before you gain, be humbled before you get promoted, or get stuck before you get free. It's all part of moving forward.

The enemy wants to narrow and warp your definition of success to discourage you. You may feel stuck in this snapshot of your life, but you are not a failure. This is not the end of your story. God uses our most significant setbacks as His greatest thrusts forward! Stuck never means stuck in the Kingdom of God!

Your Threshold

A threshold is something that must be exceeded for different conditions to occur. The word also describes the bottom of a doorway, which you must pass over to step into a new room. Both definitions paint a picture of the difference between where you are now and where you want to be. Your threshold is what you must confront or cross over to continue your forward trajectory. Said another way, it's the barrier or limiter that keeps you from transitioning into what God has for you next. Think of the threshold as the thing holding you back, keeping you stuck where you are, and preventing you from moving forward.

A practical example of a threshold is a governor on an engine. I own a utility terrain vehicle (UTV) at the family cabin that has a mechanical speed limiter that prevents it from exceeding its governed speed of 25 MPH. If you drive it fast downhill, you can feel the governor kick in to slow the UTV down. The engine is capable of 45 MPH, but the governor limits its performance to 25 MPH. We are all capable of more. We have relationships, talents, ministries, and careers that could become more than they are. So why don't they become more? Because we have thresholds in place that keep us stuck in place. Any area you feel stuck is an indication that you've come up upon a threshold.

Some of these thresholds have become ingrained in the way we think and live. We may not even recognize their existence. Just as you no longer notice the decorations on your living room wall because they are so familiar, these thresholds can feel more like familiar old friends than enemies of our progress and success.

I've had lower back pain off and on throughout my life. It's been such a regular occurrence, I've learned to incorporate it into my life, and I hardly notice it now. It limits me from lifting things and participating in activities I'd like to do but since the pain has become routine in my life, so have the limits. In a way, my back pain is a threshold. The thing that holds us back has likely become routine in our lives. We have accepted it as normal and don't recognize how it limits us.

When we come to a threshold, it represents a point of decision. Either we decide to bust through the limiter and continue growing, or we get stopped in our tracks. If we refuse to cross that threshold, life has a way of bringing us back around to face it again. We are prone to repeating our mistakes before we learn from them. Fortunately, God is a patient Teacher!

I've found most people know, deep down, they are stuck in some form or another. So, why do we remain stuck? It's one of two reasons:

1. We stay stuck because it feels safer than the unknown that exists on the other side of our threshold. Quite simply, we desire to stay with what feels familiar or safe. We want to live in a world we know, repeating the same habits we know, in relationship with the same people we know. Familiarity feels the same as control, and crossing a threshold always involves giving up some degree of control or power. Crossing a threshold feels scary because it's a risk. We are unaware of how much familiarity dictates our lives. I visit the same websites each day because I'm familiar with how to navigate them to find the information I need. I drive the same route to work each day, even though it's not the fastest or shortest route. I have a particular hotel chain I choose to stay in as often as possible because I like the predictability of having the same experience regardless of the city I'm in (okay, and I love the hotel points, too!). While there may be benefits with each of these choices, I'm not picking any of these choices solely based on what is most beneficial for my life. I'm making these choices based on what feels most familiar.
2. We stay stuck because we misdiagnose the cause of our threshold. We commonly label our threshold as our circumstances or other people, but our threshold is always something within our control. We would like to believe it's an outside force, something that is beyond our responsibility, because then we don't have to bravely face the reality that WE are the reason we are stuck. More specifically, the source of our threshold is in our thinking. This is bad news because it removes our excuses. It's good news because it empowers us to do something about it. When we misdiagnose the cause, we try to change the wrong things. It results in wasted energy and produces poor results.

Any time you encounter a threshold, it is an opportunity for you to invite Jesus into your life in a new way. This is the ultimate decision that each one of us must make for every area of our lives. I don't know everything that lies in the unknown on the other side, but I do know more of Jesus lies on the other side. You can't have more of Him without breaking through your threshold. It opens the door to new potential, new opportunities, and new ways of experiencing life.

Jesus meets us at our point of decision, waiting for us to give up control and trust Him enough to step with Him into the unknown. He won't force us over the threshold, though He may very well allow circumstances to give you a gentle (or not-so-gentle) nudge. Instead, He meets us at our threshold, ready to take the lead. Your threshold is about to become the bridge to something new, something extraordinary.

Your Tension

Believe it or not, being stuck can be a good thing. It's a crucial part of our development as humans. There is a tension when you approach a threshold that represents the point of decision or a choice you need to make regarding that threshold. In this place of tension, you choose—do I break through my threshold into a new place of thinking and living, or do I continue in my current state?

The tension is the place of struggle where you decide whether you will seek to protect and maintain your current norm or if you will take a step of courage towards a new norm. This tension may feel like restlessness, dissatisfaction, or even a midlife crisis. In this place of pressure, you decide whether to change or whether to go around the mountain again. Whether to face the pain of changing or choose the familiarity of staying miserable.

Chapter 2: We Each Have a Threshold

I began to notice this place of tension in my life long before I recognized there was a threshold keeping me stuck. For me, it was growing frustration that what I expected and what I wanted life to look like was very different than what I was experiencing. At first, I attempted to explain away, justify, and place blame for the discrepancy. But none of those things relieved the tension. If anything, they only increased my frustration. It wasn't until I recognized that the tension was a reflection of my internal belief struggle that I learned it was leading me somewhere. It was leading me forward.

The adage that we remain in our current condition until the pain of staying the same outweighs the pain of changing is true. The problem is that we often have an inadequate understanding of what our current condition is costing us. We may be ignorant to the effects of our behavior on others. We may be numb to the pain we feel because we've shoved it so far below the surface that it is out of sight. We may be unaware of the deception we believe about ourselves, God, or others. Tension is a gift because it awakens us to our reality. It awakens us from routine in the same way rumble strips on the highway awaken us from a driving lull.

We may hate the tension, but it is our friend when it comes to growth and progress. Our muscles require tension to move. Friction moves a car forward. Conflict helps relationships mature. A spiritual journey requires a struggle to build faith. Forward progress is born in places of pressure. Because we are human, we avoid discomfort at all costs and do whatever we can to get through the tension—even at the expense of our progress. Tension, or struggle, is a crucial and necessary part of growth.

One of the greatest things the Holy Spirit is teaching me is to embrace the seasons of tension and restlessness. Those seasons become a springboard for what comes next. Like an arrow pulled back, the tension of the string on the bow makes it possible to launch an arrow. These are the seasons when you want to give up the most because the pressure feels the greatest. But what comes next is always worth it. Take heart, my friend. You're about to be launched.

Your Thought Trap

This book will expound on the formation of thought traps and how to break free of them, but I want to take a moment and lay some foundation for how these traps operate in conjunction with the threshold. Wherever there is a threshold, you will find errant thinking. Your thoughts produce your emotions, which shape your behaviors, which determine your results. We frequently misdiagnose our threshold because we believe our emotions, behaviors, and results are in response to our circumstances. As a general rule of thumb, we don't get stuck in our circumstances; we get stuck in our thoughts.

Any time there is a behavior or habit you can't break, there is a thought process under the surface driving it. It is cyclical thinking resulting in cyclical behavior. On the other side of the threshold is a new way of thinking and behaving, with different results. Without crossing the threshold, the centrifugal motion of your cycle will keep you from advancing.

One day while mowing at the cabin, I raised the deck of the lawnmower so I could mow grass in an area that had rocky soil to avoid a clash between the blades and the rocks. After mowing that area, I proceeded to mow the trail around the pond. Because our trail is 10 feet wide, I make one pass around the outside of the trail and then turn around and make a second pass to mow the inner half of the trail. As I completed my initial pass and turned around, I glanced over at the half I had just cut and realized I never lowered the deck again. I had mowed the entire pass barely knocking off the top of the grass. I had put forth the activity and effort necessary to mow the path but wasn't effective in producing the desired results.

Your trap is likely a cyclical behavior and way of thinking that renders lots of activity in your life but is not effective in producing the results that will move you forward. Cyclical behavior is the equivalent of mowing the path again with the deck still up! Consider the Pharisees who excelled at spiritual busyness, all while being ineffective for the Kingdom of God. They were stuck and didn't know it! I believe millions of adults are stuck but are too busy to notice. They have lots of activity and effort directed at the wrong things. Activity is not the same as progress. *Note: Busyness is just a socially acceptable form of avoidance!*

Each one of us has habits and patterns we would like to change, but for whatever reason, we have been unable to cross the threshold. We've attempted to modify our behavior without changing its underlying cause. As Romans 12:2 says, *"Don't copy the behavior and customs of this world, but let God transform you into a new person by changing the way you think. Then you will learn to know God's will for you, which is good and pleasing and perfect."* God always transforms from the inside out to produce lasting change. He starts with your thought-life.

Your Transition

The struggle of the tension period makes you want to change, and your threshold is your decision to change. But the transition period is where you implement change. In this season, you learn how to think in new ways so you can learn to live in new ways. It is where you begin to establish new, healthier, and more effective patterns in your life.

I'm a big believer that a good pair of leather boots is worth the investment. The best boots mold to your feet the more you wear them, offering maximum support and comfort. To get unstuck, we may have to do some things that feel very unfamiliar. It's like taking home a new pair of boots. They feel unfamiliar at first because they haven't stretched to the shape of your foot. You might even find yourself tripping from time to time as you learn how to navigate with your new soles—or am I the only one who does that? Over time, you break them in and the boots become comfortable.

Any time you leave the status quo and cross your threshold, there will be a season of transition where you "break in" your new, and where things feel unnatural and uncomfortable. These transitions can be lengthy when you are breaking long-standing cycles. And like any form of transition, they can be disruptive.

One of the ways the farmers in my family prepare the ground for new growth is by tearing up the old roots of past years and the settled ground from a long winter. There is an implement they pull behind the tractor to dig up the dirt I call The Ripper. I'm sure it has a significantly more technical name, but I call it The Ripper because it looks like a row of giant claws that dig deep into the ground. It is a much deeper disruption of the land than a standard plow, but they use it since it can break up the roots and settled ground far below the surface, which is good for the long-term health of the land. The specially designed implement is for soil that hasn't been tilled in many years. Often, small trees have grown with established root systems and the ground is packed. Without digging deep and tearing through those root systems, the soil will resist new growth.

Sometimes the Lord breaks up shallow roots in our thinking, and His upheaval in our lives is uncomfortable but not disruptive.

At other times He uses The Ripper and digs deep to tear up long-established patterns of thought and behavior. This kind of digging is most painful, but the deeper the digging, the greater the opportunity to experience His love (for the Lord disciplines those He loves) and long-term fruitfulness (for the Lord prunes those He wants to be fruitful). Ultimately, the upheaval of the established ground creates an opportunity for new growth. We don't like the digging process, but it's the very process God uses to draw us closer to Him. Like so many Kingdom principles, it seems counterintuitive to me. I think He likes it that way.

At the beginning of a new planting season, you must uproot the remains of the previous season. The remnants of last year's season—even if it was a good season and you invested a lot—can never support the crop of the new year. The same is true in our lives. I know many Christians who pray for God to do a new thing, but they are unwilling to let go of the past season. People would think my dad is crazy if he thought the dead cornstalks of last year would produce new growth this year.

However, the decomposition of the former year's stalks enriches the next year's. Death in the Kingdom of God always supports new life. Perhaps we don't experience the new because we're not good at letting go of the old? We fight the upheaval process, and in doing so, we fight progress. I don't know if I'll ever grow to love the upheaval process, but I do pray that I'll learn to embrace it. How much heartache and anxiety do we cause ourselves by fighting upheaval, instead of trusting that God will never cause disruption where He doesn't intend to plant new life? It is both a spiritual principle and a principle of nature that death brings about new life. Just as a seed must die for a sprout to form, the Lord uses upheaval in us to do a new thing. To look at the broken seed, you would think it has been destroyed. But instead, it has given way to new life. The next level of your life will require a new level of you.

Jesus addressed this thinking to the followers of John the Baptist. They questioned why Jesus's disciples didn't fast according to Jewish traditions. They wanted to know why Jesus's disciples didn't behave in the way disciples always had before. He responds in Matthew 9:17, *"And no one puts new wine into old wineskins. For the old skins would burst from the pressure, spilling the wine and ruining the skins. New wine is stored in new wineskins so that both are preserved."*

This concept of new wineskins teaches us about the transition period where we move from the old to the new way of thinking. Wineskins require death, stretching, rigorous cleaning, trimming, and shaping before they are usable. We are like wineskins. A goat must die to produce a hide; we must die to our pride to produce new life in us. But this is just the beginning. A wineskin must be stretched and made pliable; He stretches us beyond our capabilities so we are pliable for His use. The skin must be thoroughly cleaned; He will clean up the cluttered areas of our hearts. The skin must be cut down to the proper shape; He cuts away relationships, attitudes, and wrong beliefs. The skin must be shaped into a container; He shapes us into the image of Christ. All of these things happen during the transition period where we are being made new.

We love the result, but we don't like to think about the work required for the end result to take place. God is a God of process, and everything He does is the result of process. The result gives purpose and perspective to the process. If you're going through a season that requires a tremendous amount of dying to self, purifying, and trimming, know that it is to shape you into a suitable vessel for the new thing God has for you. It's necessary and the end result makes the process worth it. A wineskin that hasn't been through the stretching process is unable to expand to hold new wine. To put new wine in a wineskin that hasn't been cleaned would contaminate the new wine. To put wine in a wineskin that hasn't been trimmed and shaped would make it bulky, which would diminish its usefulness to the owner.

God is active in all seasons of our lives, but there are seasons where His activity is more evident. It's easy to think that growth only happens in the spring and harvest only occurs in the fall. On the contrary, the cold winter is a valuable time of preparation for the planting season, and the hot summer is preparation for the fall. Farmers work hard in those transitional seasons to prepare their equipment, tend to their crops, and make plans for the future. A farmer wastes no season. Making the most of your current season leads to better results in the next. Fruitfulness happens because we go through the cycle of seasons. God is so interested in your fruitfulness that He, like a good farmer, wastes no season. If you are in a transitional season, God is doing something transformational to prepare you for what comes next.

These seasons of upheaval are painful and shake us to our core by design. It's easy to become mad at God, but that season of turmoil is likely the pathway to the very things your heart longs for. His upheaval isn't without purpose but instead an expression of His love and validation of your worth. Your destiny requires the kind of growth and progress that upheaval brings.

Because this part of the process carries such high stakes, I want to explain what you can expect so you'll know to push through. In many ways, this transition period feels like a secondary threshold because you may question your decision to change, and you will be tempted to slip back into old ways of thinking. I tell you this so you won't be surprised when it comes, the same way a nurse tells you a shot is going to sting before poking you with a needle. Knowing what kinds of pain may lie ahead empowers you to recognize it when it happens and know it's normal. Four common painful aspects of transition are detachment, disorientation, disillusionment, and discouragement. You can anticipate any or all of these experiences as part of your process.

Detachment (Grief)

Sometimes God invites us into the next season by opening a door in front of us, allowing us to embrace what comes next. Sometimes God invites us into the next season by closing doors behind us, asking us to let go of what we've known. Either way, you must grieve what was so you can embrace what is to come.

When we cling with a tight grip to the very thing God wants us to leave behind, it comes at the expense of our future. Ecclesiastes 3:6 says there is a time to keep and a time to throw away, and Isaiah 43:18 instructs us to forget the former things so we can embrace the new thing God is doing. This doesn't mean we forget that something happened or that we dishonor the past. It simply means we must be more committed to what comes next than we are to the past.

Disorientation (Confusion)

When you break free from a former way of thinking, you will see and experience your life in different ways. It feels confusing when your belief system is challenged. Since we use those beliefs as a compass for life, we feel unsettled when our beliefs are upended. It can be a fearful thing to discover the world is different than you believed!

In my softball days, I played shortstop. When a runner attempts to steal second base, the shortstop generally covers the bag so the catcher can throw the ball in an attempt to beat the runner to the base. The first thing they teach a shortstop about covering second base is to go to the bag first and then focus on catching the ball and tagging the runner. The base orients you, allowing you to catch the ball and apply a quick tag. It becomes a point of reference for responding to both the ball and the runner.

When we go through seasons of disruption, the people and perspectives we used as points of reference often change. We may feel like we've "lost our bearings," and aspects of life feel unfamiliar to us or may even feel out of control. You may find in this place that you can't trust your feelings or your own judgment. It is during this transition period that you must become reoriented around who God is and who He says you are. In essence, He becomes your point of reference for how you interpret and respond to what is happening around you.

Disillusionment (Disappointment)

Disillusionment is when you realize something is not what you thought it was. It's a combination of disappointment in another person and frustration with yourself for not recognizing it sooner. It's a painful realization to see just how much your skewed version of reality has misled you. Perhaps what you thought was true isn't, the people you thought were for you ended up betraying you, or the things you thought made you happy were the very things holding you back.

You may ask yourself questions like, "How did I not see who that person *really* was?" "Why did I let them walk all over me for so long?" or "How did I not see how my behavior was affecting others?" My experiences with disillusionment have left me feeling disappointed in myself and others.

It's important to recognize disillusionment when it occurs. Knowing this is what you are experiencing helps you manage the disorientation with wisdom and respond with balanced measures. For example, disillusionment may help us see someone else's behavior is not as loving as we thought but is instead manipulative and self-serving. Our fleshly reaction is to cut them out of our lives entirely (and in some circumstances, this may be entirely appropriate and healthy). We are tempted to react this way because we cannot separate our pain from disillusionment and the behavior of the person. It feels one and the same. This natural reaction is not entirely negative, as it can help you be brave in setting new boundaries and establishing new ways of relating. The effects of disillusionment are often like a pendulum. You will swing from one extreme to the next, but you will generally fall back into balance as you sort out truth and gain new perspective.

Discouragement (Hopelessness)

You will experience resistance any time you make changes in your life. Resistance is pushback or reaction to what we do. When I was young, waterbeds were popular. I can remember what it felt like to plop down on my oldest brother's waterbed and feel the water respond to the weight of my body. It was a ripple effect (literally!). The same thing happens when we change our behaviors. It causes a ripple effect, often one that tries to push us back to the status quo. This will come from your own soul, which loves familiarity. Resistance can also come from people in your life, as not everyone wants you to change because if you change your patterns, it affects their patterns.

Resistance will most certainly come from the enemy, and it primarily comes in the form of discouragement. His goal is to get you to retreat and go back to the way things used to be, even more defeated and ashamed. Discouragement is the lie of the enemy that your circumstances can't or won't change. It's normal to begin making a change, experience the discomfort of the change, and wish to turn back!

Adding to this, the enemy wants you to feel ashamed, defeated, and hopeless. These emotions rob you of the energy and courage needed to get and stay unstuck. The enemy wants you to believe this transition period IS your breakthrough. He wants you to believe the lie that it's not worth it to continue. He wants you to give up and fall back into the patterns of thinking and behavior that got you stuck in the first place. You will need to push through these emotions to get your breakthrough.

So, are you ready to get unstuck?

The zero-turn mower has tires with minimal tread. This is what allows me to drive it like a race car, turning and spinning at will, without tearing up the ground. It's convenient when I'm on dry land. However, when I'm stuck in wet ground, it renders the tires completely useless. If I try to accelerate to get myself unstuck, the smooth-faced tires only spin me into a deeper state of being stuck! The phrase "spinning your wheels" means lots of effort with no results. I'm sure there have been times you have felt stuck, and everything you do to try to get unstuck only digs you deeper into your situation. It's time to stop spinning and start surrendering.

The good news for believers is that we have a God who is more invested in you becoming unstuck than you are. Think of the Old Testament—it's the story of how God's chosen people get stuck, get unstuck, get stuck, get unstuck, over and over. You might say that God has a long track record of helping people become unstuck. But that's not all. When you jump to the New

Testament, you find that God provided the ultimate way to become unstuck in the person of Jesus. Are you stuck in sin? Jesus brings forgiveness. Are you stuck in shame? Jesus brings freedom. Stuck in addiction? Jesus offers a way out. Stuck in conflict? Jesus is the ultimate mediator. Stuck in indecision? Jesus lights the way. There is no condition of being stuck that Jesus can't help you overcome. You can spin your wheels by trying to do it on your own, or you can invite the all-powerful and ever-present Savior of the world to come and meet you in your place of stuck. He waits at your threshold, ready to lead you on.

PART TWO

Why We Get and Stay Stuck

CHAPTER 3

OUR THRESHOLD IS IN OUR THINKING

I have a chihuahua mix dog I adopted from an animal shelter several years ago. Like most chihuahuas, she is full of personality, odd quirks, and "little dog syndrome." Her bark truly is bigger than her bite, but she doesn't know that. Her name is Specimen B, which only adds to her uniqueness. I had a lapse in judgment back in my youth ministry days and let teenagers name her. Fortunately, she doesn't seem to mind.

One day, I took Specimen B (B for short) and Sadie (my original dog—nicknamed by the teenagers as Specimen A) on a walk after work. In their excitement to meet me at the door where I was waiting with their leashes, Sadie, a black lab mix, bumped into the broom leaning up against my wall and knocked it over. It fell on the floor, the handle blocking the path from my kitchen to my living room. I left the house without giving it a second thought. When we returned from the walk, I took off their leashes and went to sit down on my couch to do some super-spiritual activity (okay, I'm pretty sure I was watching TV). After a few minutes, I heard a whimper from the other room. I looked up to see B standing on the other side of the broom. She refused to cross the handle to come into the room with me and was calling for my help. I had a good laugh and picked up the broom so she could sit on the couch by me. Here's my point—B could easily step over that broom, but her thinking about the handle was faulty. It seemed like a barrier or a threat. Her threshold wasn't the broom; it was her thinking about the broom. To conquer our threshold, we must confront our thinking.

We have to go below the surface.

A few years ago, when I was a new homeowner, I was anxious to renovate my house. My kitchen had original 1970s olive green appliances, and my basement still had hideous shag carpet! Unfortunately, I wanted an HGTV house on a yard sale budget. In my early stages of renovations, I admittedly cut corners to get the job done. Sure, I wanted to ensure things were done right, but I was most concerned about aesthetics. When it came time to renovate my bathroom, I found a great deal on a new bathtub that allowed me to spend money on tile instead. I didn't consider the long-term implications of choosing the cheaper bathtub. Fast forward 10 years and the tub has begun to show signs of wear and cracking. To replace the tub, I will also have to replace all of that beautiful tile!

There is an undeniable appeal to cheap bathtubs, fast fixes, get-rich-quick schemes, and crash diets. All offer a temporary fix without addressing the underlying issues that caused the problem in the first place. Unfortunately, there's no easy shortcut for getting unstuck. If it were easy to get unstuck, you would have done it already. Your "stuckness" is likely the result of something buried deep within you, and it will take some work to uncover it and deal with it. Being stuck doesn't happen on the surface; it happens far below the surface, often out of sight.

Since we get stuck under the surface, we must go below the surface and beyond the obvious to get unstuck. An iceberg is an iconic illustration of how what is unseen relates to what is seen. It applies here, as well. We think we are stuck in our repeated behaviors and their outcomes, but we're actually stuck far below the surface. This is what makes it so hard to identify and fix the places we are stuck in. This is also why Satan wages war against our thoughts.

BENEATH THE SURFACE

RESULTS	
	Where we think we are stuck
BEHAVIORS	
FEELINGS	
THOUGHTS	Where we are actually stuck

The more I talk to people about getting unstuck, the more I see that everything comes back to one thing—our thinking. Buried within our thinking processes is a threshold that holds us back. This threshold is a particular way of thinking that limits our ability to change or move forward.

Paul describes this thought threshold in Romans 7:18 (NLT), *"And I know that nothing good lives in me, that is, in my sinful nature. I want to do what is right, but I can't."* Though Paul wanted to be victorious over his sinful nature, his desire to change behaviors wasn't enough. There was something deeper within him that was at war with his mind and was a threshold to his growth. His threshold was in his thinking. He goes on in verses 22–23 to say, *"I love God's law with all my heart. But there is another power within me that is at war with my mind. This power makes me a slave to the sin that is still within me."* The word "war" isn't referencing a singular battle but an ongoing campaign to destroy him. The term "slave" describes a captive of war. The enemy is relentless in his campaign against your thoughts, and his ultimate goal is to make you a prisoner to sin and a slave to your threshold. Make no mistake, there is an ongoing battle for your thought-life.

Likely you can relate to Paul. Perhaps you desire to lose weight, but you eat fast food anyway. You want to be confident, but you let your insecurities hold you back. You want to forgive, but you just can't seem to move on. If you wish to do one thing but continually do the opposite, you are stuck in your thinking. We may not be able to change our circumstances, and we certainly can't change other people (trust me, I've tried), but we CAN change our thinking.

Another way to think of this concept is to consider the process from thought to outcome. We spend a great deal of time in discipleship talking about the results a believer should have, and we paint a clear picture of the behaviors a believer should have. We even tell others what to think, but we often fall short in teaching people *how* to think. We get it backward. We hope that by simply modifying our behaviors, we can change our results. But as Paul discovered, the war in our minds is stronger than our efforts to improve.

We like a version of "truth" that fits into our existing narrative, doesn't challenge our beliefs, and doesn't require us to change. But real truth does all of these things. David says in Psalm 139:23–24, "*Search me, O God, and know my heart; test me and know my anxious thoughts. Point out anything in me that offends you, and lead me along the path of everlasting life.*" If you want to get unstuck, you must invite the Holy Spirit to search and examine what lies below the surface.

Our thoughts often evade us.

We can identify the results of being stuck and may recognize the behaviors that lead to those results, but diagnosing the thoughts that drive those behaviors and results can be much more evasive. This is because our thoughts are often unconscious and therefore go unchecked. To be honest, we don't think about our thoughts very often. Ironic, isn't it?

We are often unaware of the framework that shapes our thoughts, emotions, and behaviors. Because so much of our thinking is subconscious and cyclical, it does not get examined regularly. 1 Chronicles 28:9 says, "*…for the LORD searches all hearts and understands all the intent of the thoughts. If you seek Him, He will be found by you….*" The word "intent" means the framing of the mind. It represents the underlying beliefs that serve as the framework for the way we think and respond to our world. A framework is a basic structure of an object. You generally can't see the framework of something because it's covered or concealed. If there's an issue with the framework, it can only be addressed by exposing the framework. You cannot get unstuck without exposing the belief systems and thought processes that got you stuck in the first place.

These thoughts can be buried beneath the emotions we don't want to feel. For example, the pain of feeling inadequate can be overwhelming, so we avoid feeling it altogether. This means we also avoid examining the thoughts that go with it. It's scary to go below the surface.

Some friends of mine purchased a century-old house with lots of character and lots of potential for sweat equity. Every simple project turns into a bigger, more expensive one once they tear something out and see what they are truly dealing with. Recently, they discovered a portion of their house had been fixed incorrectly by the previous owner, leading to damage to the siding. The husband, daunted by the thought of what might be beneath the surface, said, "I'm not sure I want to tear that off because I don't know what I'll find." I can relate to that sentiment with my thought-life! But I love how his wife responded, "How can you not? It's rotten!" Often, our thoughts evade us because we don't want to know what might be below the surface. The denial of their existence doesn't negate their effects any more than ignoring the issues on the house made the problems go away. If you're unsure about taking this journey to get unstuck in your thought-life, I ask you, "How can you not? It's rotten!" By the way, my friends went on to fix the roof, and, as a result of all the projects they have tackled, their house is worth significantly more. It pays off to go beneath the surface!

We can't believe what we think or feel.

There are two things I hate about flying. The first thing is flight delays, which have taught me a great deal about letting go of things outside of my control and a great deal about exercising the fruit of the Spirit! The second is the turbulence. Bear in mind, I hate roller coasters and can get sick on a swing if I'm not careful. Turbulence is not my friend! I don't mind the normal bumps of flying through unpredictable air. It's the times when it feels like you are suddenly dropping out of the sky that gets my heart (and imagination) racing. I'm the passenger who grabs the armrest with white knuckles and starts praying under my breath when turbulence hits. I've even envisioned how I would lead the entire plane in an alter call for mass salvation while we plummet to certain death!

I FEEL like the plane is falling from the sky (well, my stomach does, at least). In addition to being a savvy flyer, I'm also a savvy Googler, so I know that the typical terrifying drop in the sky is usually only a few feet at most. And I KNOW that turbulence is rarely dangerous. I have the information I need to feel differently, and yet I still have anxiety about it. My fear of turbulence comes from my inaccurate conclusions or beliefs about what is happening. My experience is real, but not based on reality. My emotions come from my belief framework about what is happening, not my knowledge.

If you feel stuck in life, there is likely an inaccurate conclusion (lie) at the root of it all. There is a thought process keeping you in your rut. There is a fault in your framework. A wrong belief is keeping you from moving forward. Specimen B was stuck because of her thoughts about the broom handle, not because of the actual broom. This is a foundational truth we must understand if we want to become unstuck, and it is not an easy one because it requires us first to admit our blame for why we are stuck (unfair circumstances, incompetent people, etc.) is wrong. Our thinking is the culprit, and that can be changed!

The trickiest thing about the lies we believe is that we often do not know the lies are a lie. Satan is very cunning and loves to masquerade his thoughts as our own. Any lie he convinces us to believe is rooted in some element of truth. When a plane experiences turbulence, the truth is the plane drops. But the truth becomes warped into a lie when my mind convinces me the drop is much more significant than it is. I hate turbulence, but turbulence isn't the problem. My thinking is.

Our thoughts and feelings can lead us to the truth.
Emotions tell us what lies below the surface. They act much like the warning lights on your car dashboard, indicating when something is wrong. For this reason, emotions are helpful in leading us to the things we need to see under the surface. For example, we may not realize we believe a lie, but we might recognize the presence of fear or anxiety. Emotions tell us what we really believe.

In my early 20s, I noticed a recurring theme where I struggled to fall asleep on Saturday nights. I'd often toss and turn until two or three in the morning. After months of this pattern, I asked the Lord to show me what was going on. He revealed that my sleeplessness was due to anxiety about being on stage every Sunday morning for the worship team. Once I became aware of those emotions, it was easy to see there was fear tied to my thoughts below the surface. I was able to surrender my perfectionism and fear of failure, and I've slept like a baby on Saturday nights ever since!

Jesus wants to be the Lord of all of us—body, soul, and spirit. He's not interested in a fragmented lordship. The cross invites us to bring our thoughts and feelings into submission to the truth so that we can think, feel, and live according to the truth. This submission is how we begin to break free from our cycles and align our emotions with the heart of the Father.

Our thoughts matter in the Kingdom of God.

Matthew 9 tells the story of Jesus healing a paralyzed man. After restoring his ability to walk and forgiving his sins, Jesus was accused of blasphemy by the religious leaders. From their perspective, only God could forgive and they did not believe Jesus was God. His response to their accusations tells us something important about His priorities. Instead of confronting what they say, Jesus confronts their wrong thinking in Matthew 9:4 "*But Jesus, knowing their thoughts, said, 'Why do you think evil in your hearts?'*" What a fascinating response! Their anger (emotion) revealed their thinking. Jesus goes under the surface because He knows how much our thoughts affect our lives. In this case, it wasn't the religious leaders' words or actions that kept them from experiencing Jesus, but their thinking.

God is keenly interested in the quality of your thoughts because He cares about the quality of your fruit. The Gospel invites us into a different way of living—one that is marked by a different way of thinking. The thoughts we have govern our emotions. The emotions we feel determine the behaviors we choose. The behaviors we choose determine the results we achieve. This graphic shows how the seeds in our thought-lives determine the fruit we produce.

PROGRESSION OF A THOUGHT

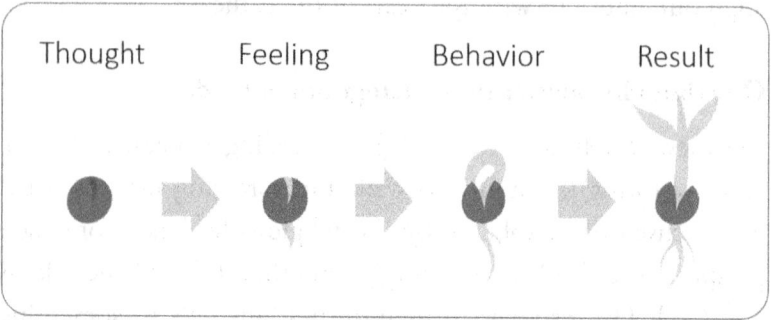

Colossians 3:10 says, *"Put on your new nature, and be renewed as you learn to know your Creator and become like him."* The word "renew" here means to make new by completing a process. It means to make fresh or new by completing a process that can only be achieved by God's power. It is similar to the word "renovate" in the English language. This isn't the kind of renovation where you slap some new paint on walls. Instead, it's the kind where you tear the walls down to the studs and start again. It's a systematic demolishing and rebuilding of our thought-life.

Several years ago, I decided to renovate my kitchen. I can remember being halfway into demolition and looking around at the mess. Everything was covered in drywall dust, and the entire contents of my kitchen cabinets were scattered throughout my house. It was overwhelming, and I'll admit, I questioned whether the mess was worth it! Eventually, the mess was cleaned up, and the kitchen was rebuilt. Custom-made cabinets and countertops were installed, giving my pots and pans a home once again. After seeing the fruit of the rebuilding process, I knew it was worth it.

Our lives are the sum of our thoughts, so each thought matters. We can expect a mess when He breaks down old thoughts and repairs what is broken. But it will be worth it when we emerge more beautiful, purposeful, and useful for His Kingdom.

A lie we believe is the root of every reason we get stuck.

What is broken in our "framework" of thinking is the lies we believe. Each one of us has inaccurate conclusions we've formed about ourselves, others, our circumstances, and God. These inaccurate conclusions aren't a representation of the truth, but rather a subtle deception we've adopted as truth. It's incredibly humbling, even humiliating, to admit you believe a lie. After all, our pride is convinced we've mastered truth. But as we'll learn in the next chapter, truth takes root in the soil of humility. Admitting your deception is the first step to gaining truth.

For every area of your life where a threshold exists, that threshold has power in your life because it is fueled by a lie. When we remove the lie, we remove the threshold. It sounds simple… and so did my kitchen renovation project at first! In reality, it's a messy process and will require a complete renovation of the way you think. It will be worth the mess and disruption, I promise.

CHAPTER 4

THE NATURE OF TRUTH

Sometimes the best way to define something is to clarify what it is not, as the contrast enhances our understanding. To learn how believing a lie can get us stuck, let's first examine its counterpart—truth.

The more familiar we become with truth, the more equipped we will be in detecting lies. It's like seeing someone in Iowa with a great tan in January— you know it's not the real deal. Think of it this way: Deception happens in the absence of truth. This is why there is such a battle to keep you from knowing the truth. When we don't fill our souls with truth, the enemy fills that vacuum with lies.

I had a friend in college who accidentally filled her car with diesel fuel instead of gasoline. Because the manufacturer built her engine for gas, it had damaging and expensive results. Our Designer created us to run on truth, but the enemy wants us to fill up on other things.

The world teaches us that truth is relative, subjective, and something you must define for yourself. It tells us truth must be politically correct, but this kind of "truth" is as cheap as the next opinion. Furthermore, the very idea of truth is compromised by photoshopped magazine covers, dishonest media, and arrogant educational systems. These things are false representations of truth the enemy uses to fill our vacuum. They can't be trusted.

This is a far cry from the truth described in the Bible. Real truth is absolute and does not change with the winds of culture. All truth comes from God, and all truth leads us to Him. There is no truth apart from Him, and this is what our souls crave and need. It is truth that can be trusted.

We learn a lot about the nature of truth from Jesus in John 8 when He addresses Pharisees who were twisting the Law to trap Him. This confrontation with the Pharisees follows the encounter Jesus had with the woman caught in adultery. Jesus spares this woman from death and now flips the script on those trying to stone her. The rationale for their judgmental and hypocritical actions came from their version of the truth—a version devoid of mercy. As Psalm 85:10 (NKJV) says, *"Mercy and truth have met together; righteousness and peace have kissed."* Truth, in its fullness, brings into harmony both mercy and truth. The Pharisees had a misrepresentation or distortion of the truth that served their needs. In short form, they believed and were bound by a lie that prevented them from experiencing the personhood of Jesus (and, consequently, caused them to miss the Kingdom value of the adulterous woman).

Characteristics of Truth

① Truth is our optimal operating system.

For my 37th birthday, I bought an expensive memory foam bed. For my 37th Christmas, I bought myself a new laptop. Yep, I'm that exciting. I can remember when my family purchased our first computer back in the early '90s. The operating system was MS-DOS, and the letters on the screen were green. We thought it was so cool! We've come a long way with our operating systems since then! Today, computer operating systems allow us to do some remarkable things. The operating system is the "thinking" system of the machine, allowing it to perform a wide range of functions. My laptop is designed for a particular operating system and would be useless without it.

We have a redemptive identity as children of God—the highest calling and identity possible. Truth, as an operating system, is what enables us to fulfill that design. When we live in truth, we live as God created us to be. When we work off of a faulty operating system (lies) we get less-than-optimal results. If I were to uninstall my laptop's operating system and install a 1990s version of DOS, I wouldn't be able to do much beyond a game of Oregon Trail! The Pharisees in John 8 were living out of a faulty operating system, one which caused them to misinterpret what Jesus was doing in their midst. There are many times in my life I've missed what He was doing for the same reason.

Psalm 51:6 (NKJV) says, *"You desire truth in the inward parts, and in the hidden part You will make me know wisdom."* The "inward parts" represent what isn't seen initially and the "hidden part" is a place we have kept shut up or concealed. For truth to be our operating system, we must invite truth below the surface.

② Truth longs to make its home in you.

In John 8:31, Jesus says, *"You are truly my disciples if you remain faithful to my teachings."* The word "faithful" means to stay, abide, remain. The Bible has much to say about this concept of abiding. Think of abiding as settling in and making your home in a place.

One of the first things I do when I arrive at a hotel is to untuck the sheets on the bed. It sounds weird, but I can't stand feeling trapped when I'm sleeping. Why do I do this? Because it makes it feel like home and allows me to settle in and relax. When I abide in Christ, I settle in and make my home in truth.

Your home is the center of your life's activity. To abide is to establish the center of your life in Jesus, where your life flows out of Him. Many Christians are content to visit, but Jesus wants you to untuck the sheets and make yourself at home. There is both longevity and intimacy implied. When we make our home in Truth and build our lives within it, we become an expression of that truth. Our abiding becomes our expression.

I'm not a neat freak, but I take pride in keeping my home picked up. If you were to drop by randomly, there's a good chance you would find my house in a relatively clean state. I would invite you in and gladly show you my living room, dining room, kitchen, main bathroom, and if I know you well enough, maybe even my bedroom. But I have one room that is always the last to be cleaned. It's my spare bedroom at the end of the hall. I call it my guest bedroom, but it tends to be more of an "I'm not sure where to keep this, so I'll just put it in my guest bedroom" room. You know how we all have a catch-all junk drawer where we put all the random stuff that doesn't have a defined home elsewhere? This room is a junk drawer in room form.

The public spaces of my house are kept clean, just in case you stop by. But that room gets neglected because I know no one is going to see it. It's easy to justify or overlook. It's easy to shut the door and pretend the mess isn't there. The same thing holds in our lives. Sometimes we allow "truth" to invade our lives just enough to clean us up for public viewing. But we're not brave enough to allow truth to invade the parts of our lives we keep from everyone else. There are areas of our hearts that we closed the door on years ago—maybe even with lock and key. It's like we keep a junk drawer in our hearts, where we put things we can't process, don't want to feel, or are covered with shame. I also know that my house is only as clean as that bedroom is. In reality, I've just consolidated my mess to one place. It's not less mess; it's just a hidden mess. Because I've hidden it, I have a false sense that I've taken care of business, all while holding on to the clutter.

Religion is effective at helping people clean up their public spaces so we look clean and appear to be holy, but true discipleship is allowing truth to access all the rooms of our hearts. It is inviting truth to settle in and make itself at home in even the messiest parts. God wants all of our hearts, even the parts we don't like. The extent to which I allow His truth to do so will be the extent to which I can be transformed. Any area I withhold from Him cannot be transformed.

Some of us have allowed the truth to invade parts of our lives, while we keep the door tightly shut in other areas. And if I had to guess, I would say the area you are stuck in just might be a door you've kept closed. I *want* to clean and organize my spare bedroom. It's not a lack of desire that keeps me from doing it. It's because I feel overwhelmed when I look at the stuff I have in there. I don't know what to do with some of it. Other piles are gifts that I don't want, but I feel bad about throwing them away. I'm keeping the stack of jeans I have in there, just in case I get back to that size again. I have valid reasons for keeping the stuff, but even my legitimate reasons are keeping me from cleaning the room so that it can be used for its original purpose. My desire to have a clean room must become more significant than my desire to hang on to my stuff. And the only way to clean the space is to take care of the clutter, one piece at a time.

Perhaps you're overwhelmed by what you might find in your heart if you allow Jesus to come in and help you clean. Maybe you don't know how to process emotions like grief, regret, or guilt. Or perhaps you have legitimate reasons you want to hang on to your junk. But can I tell you something? We only resist the cleaning "process" because we underestimate the joy and freedom of the finished product. As Jesus helps you clean your heart, one piece at a time, His truth is made at home in your heart.

③ Our behavior reveals our "truth."

Jesus tells His followers that others would know they are His disciples by the way they remain faithful to His truth. We live out our truth, regardless of whether it is real truth or a lie we believe is true. If our "truth" is fear-based, we live out fear. If our "truth" is that we are the center of the world (narcissistic thinking), these beliefs find their voice in selfish and destructive behavior. But if we're living in God's truth, our lives reflect this. For example, the fruit of the Spirit is the purest expression of truth in our life. If our reaction to a situation is anything but love, joy, peace, gentleness, and self-control, then truth isn't guiding our behavior. 1 John 3:18 says, *"Dear children, let's not merely say that we love each other; let us show the truth by our actions."* The way you live serves as proof of your discipleship, and the patterns of your behavior tell a clear story about your beliefs.

Jesus confronts these Pharisees to tell them their behavior resembles the father of lies. He boldly confronts the threshold in their thinking as an act of grace, providing a way for them to change and embrace truth. Consider your behaviors in the area you feel stuck. What beliefs lie below the surface of those behaviors? When we exchange those beliefs for His Truth, our actions will soon follow suit. Real transformation happens below the surface and bears fruit in our behavior.

Jesus explains this principle in Matthew 7:20, *"Yes, just as you can identify a tree by its fruit, so you can identify people by their actions."* The seed planted below the surface grows the tree. The roots below the surface determine the health and quality of the fruit produced by the tree. An unhealthy root system grows weak fruit. Likewise, unhealthy thinking systems produce weak fruit in our lives. What happens below the surface determines what the plant above the surface produces. If your behavior is producing subpar results in your life, it's revealing what you truly believe.

4. **Truth disciplines us.**

A "disciple" is a student, so a disciple of Jesus is a student of the truth. Interestingly, both "disciple" and "discipline" come from the root word that means "to learn." Discipline is not punishment, which is an external response to something that has happened. Instead, it is the result of truth being revealed and applied from the inside out. It happens when we allow truth to train and correct us. Believers who love truth will embrace its discipline, even when it's uncomfortable and inconvenient.

We get stuck in our discipleship when we avoid the discipline of truth. Discipline and discipleship go hand-in-hand. Discipline is painful, but it is always for our good. It is the very process by which truth becomes a reality in our lives. I know from personal experience, there will be discipline in the process of getting unstuck because God wants to teach and train us in the process. Transformation is His goal.

If we are not diligent in remaining a student of the truth, we will quickly become a slave to deception. We like to believe there is a neutral gray area between truth and deception, and our pride convinces us we can live in the gray zone without any negative impact on our lives. This false belief is deception on two levels. First, it is a lie to believe there exists a gray area between truth and deceit. Something either aligns with the Word, or it doesn't. For the issues the Bible does not explicitly address, the principles of truth outlined in the Word can be applied to provide a clear picture of right and wrong. Secondly, it is a lie to believe we can live outside of the truth and not experience negative impacts. We may be unaware of the effects, but this does not negate their reality. Deception always has a steep cost, both in the present world and in eternity. If we understood just how deep and wide its effects are, we wouldn't be so passive in our treatment of it!

5. **Truth is made real to us through experience.**

John 8:32 continues, *"And you will know the truth, and the truth will set you free."* This word "know" describes a knowledge that only comes from experience. It's more than information or logic. It is knowledge that has become truth because it has been tried and tested by experience. It's truth you can build your life upon. There is no area of your life where His truth won't work. I can't think of a situation in my life where I applied the truth found in Scripture and regretted it. That doesn't mean things went my way or that I saw the result I wanted right away. It does mean I've learned, through experience, that I can count on His truth to do its work in my life.

One aspect of my job is visiting hotels before contracting to ensure they deliver the kind of service and experience my company wants to give our event attendees. If you've ever perused a hotel's website, you will notice they use professional photography and choose careful angles to capture images of their sleeping rooms and public spaces to make them appear as appealing as possible. From my experience, some hotels live up to their pictures, and some don't. Often, the only way to tell the difference is to experience the hotel in person. The images become validated (or invalidated) by experience. The Word gives us a picture of what our lives can be, and the Gospel invites us to experience those realities.

That picture becomes experiential knowledge when we apply it to situations and see the truth in action. For example, when we choose to walk in forgiveness according to the Word and experience the freedom that follows, the truth becomes real to us in a new way. Every time we experience the reality of Scripture, it has the power to displace lies we believe. This is why it is so important that we not only read the Word but act on what we learn. James 1:22 sums it up well, *"But be doers of the word, and not hearers only, deceiving yourselves."* Could it be that we live in deception, not because we don't know the Word, but because we don't apply the Word?

The enemy robs us of experiential truth by lying to us about our experiences. He doesn't want us to know how thoroughly good God is, so he distorts our perception of reality. Colossians 3:1–2 says, *"Since you have been raised to new life with Christ, set your sights on the realities of heaven, where Christ sits in the place of honor at God's right hand. Think about the things of heaven, not the things of earth."* The word "reality" is interchangeable with "truth." Paul admonishes us to see things from a heavenly perspective, which means experiencing our lives according to the reality of heaven. As we see things from His perspective, we come to know His truth. As we come to know His truth, we see and experience life from His perspective.

In Biblical days, becoming the disciple of a teacher meant you took on their mannerisms, mimicked the way they spoke, and imitated the way they behaved. They not only became a pupil of that person's teachings, but of that person himself. It was a relationship that made discipleship more than a scholarly activity and instead something that permeated the way you thought and lived. Discipleship shaped your life through experiential relationship.

As a disciple of Jesus, I not only study what He teaches, but I become a pupil of who He is. Truth is more than teaching about Jesus; it IS Jesus (John 14:6)! A person can study the teachings of Jesus for years and amass vast knowledge, but it is only through a relationship with Him that the truth becomes transformational. As a disciple of Jesus, my life becomes shaped around who He is. And it is by living life with Truth that truth becomes my operating system.

6 Truth anchors you to God's reality.

An illusion is something that seems real but is not. It is much like the tricks our eyes play on us on a hot summer day when we are out for a drive. When we look at the pavement off in the distance, the surface appears to be liquid. The mirage is caused by the refraction of sunlight, causing our eyes to perceive the pavement differently than it is.

The enemy wants you to believe an illusion about your circumstances, so he seeks to distort your perception of what is happening. How many times have you left a conversation with an understanding of what was said, only to find that the other person left with a completely different understanding? It could be that you're a terrible listener, but it could also be the enemy working to distort conversations and create division.

Chapter 4: The Nature of Truth

The truth of a situation is discovered by seeking Jesus's perspective. He is the eyewitness whose account is never biased, and His recollection is never fuzzy. His account is always trustworthy and always devoid of accusation. And here's a hint: His truth is often contrary to what you feel or see.

One of the ways I relax is by fishing on one of my family's ponds. We have a johnboat that is small enough that I can take it out on the water by myself, but big enough that it becomes unwieldy on a windy day. Once I find a spot where the fish are biting, I throw an anchor into the water. Why do I do that? Because if I don't, my boat will be at the mercy of the wind and waves. Ephesians 4:14 illustrates this well when it compares people who lack truth to being tossed about by waves. If you build your life on an illusion, you'll always be at the mercy of that illusion, just as a boat is at the mercy of the waves. Truth anchors us and keeps us from drifting away from God's reality and plan for our lives. It gives us a solid point of reference to determine how to respond to a situation and a framework for processing the world around us.

⑦ Truth always leads you toward freedom.

Giving Specimen B and Sadie baths is always quite the ordeal. First of all, they never think they need it—particularly if they have worked extra hard on their scent (usually by rolling on a dead animal). Like any good parent, I start with a calm, soothing voice as I convince them one by one to jump into the bathtub. When that doesn't work, I try my most stern dog mom voice. When that still doesn't work, I end up bribing them (don't judge me, you do it too!). But you would never know how much they detest baths by watching what happens after they are clean. The moment I finish towel drying them and let them go, they run out of my bathroom, tear up and down the hall, jump up and down off the couch, and roll all around on my rug. It's utter chaos! My dogs rarely seem more joyful and excited than they do those few moments right after a bath. Never mind that they then spend the next hour erasing some of my hard work by licking themselves clean. Anyway, I think that's a perfect illustration of what it means to be set free. We may not enjoy the process of getting clean, but once we're clean and we've become free from something that has weighed us down for years, we can't help but be filled with joy. Freedom and joy go hand in hand (or paw in paw?).

In Psalm 119:45, David says, *"I will walk in freedom, for I have devoted myself to your commands."* Truth liberates us from the lies we've believed about ourselves, freeing us to become the people God created us to be. Yet so many people are content not to be free. Most have carried the burden of deception for so long they can't remember what it was like to be free. They've worried for so long they can't remember what it's like to have a mind at peace. They've strived for so long that they can't remember what it feels like to rest. They've been entangled in sin for so long they don't know the freedom that comes with godly living.

Surely Jesus is saddened by our burdened state far more than we are, for He sees it for what it is. His yoke is easy, and His burden is light. The promise that His truth will free you from anything and everything that burdens your mind is an open invitation to all. The yoke of deception is anything but easy and light. It's oppressive and defeating. It robs you of joy and freedom. It's a yoke of bondage that robs you of the delight of being who God created you to be.

We purchased a three-year-old aspen tree for the cabin several years ago. It came in a three-gallon plastic pot, and when we removed the tree, we found that it was severely root bound. Due to the size of the container, the roots had grown in circles around the interior. The mass of roots was congested and intertwined. You cannot take a root-bound plant in its current state and expect it to thrive. The root system is everything for the tree. It is in the tree's best interest to deal with the bound roots, so a good gardener takes the sharp edge of a shovel or pruning shears and aggressively cuts at the root ball until the roots can spread. It seems cruel, even counterproductive, and yet it is necessary. And as is often true in life, the initial product seems messier than the original.

Many of us are bound by the ways we think. Lies have become intertwined with our reality to the point that we can't separate one from the other. If the Lord is cutting you deeply, it is only so you can be free to grow exponentially. The most hurtful experiences in my life have taught me the most about truth. Each time, it has felt like a shovel was chipping away at my belief systems and thought processes. I have a mentor who often says to me, "Pain is the greatest teacher." Though I grimace a bit when she says it, the principle resonates deeply. God doesn't waste pain. Instead, He makes the most of our pain by using it to teach, train, and move us forward. Seeing pain in this way doesn't take away the sting, but it does give us hope. It brings an eternal perspective to a temporary sorrow. It offers a promise to the messy process and gives pain a redemptive purpose.

Furthermore, we learn the deepest truths of God's heart when we experience the deepest pain in ours. I wish there was a shortcut or an easier way, but I haven't found it yet. During a difficult season, I can remember feeling incredibly vulnerable before the Lord with my pain. I pictured myself lying on an operating table, with my wounds fully exposed to a surgeon. I knew this represented surrender, and I knew the Lord was showing me just how deep His work in my life was. He was cutting at my roots, bringing healing and freedom. As this revelation began to bring peace to my hurting and confused soul, the Lord spoke to me. He said, "Some wounds are life giving. Just as a surgeon makes a wound to save a life, I can use even the wounds others inflict by making them My own wounds and giving them a redemptive purpose. You can trust My wounding." It was at that moment that I chose to stop fighting the surgeon's hand and instead surrender to it.

I don't know about you, but I have often fought the very process that would bring me healing. I like the idea of freedom but resist the process required to attain it. It's the equivalent of the tree saying, "Hey, don't cut my roots, I'd rather stay pot-bound!" In the Kingdom of God, pain is life giving—but only if we submit to the process.

8 Pride resists truth.

The thing about that root-bound tree is that it doesn't realize it's root bound. That's all it has ever known. When we've been stuck for years, we may not recognize that we're bound. Pride prevents us from seeing our need for pruning and cutting. We may not realize we have stopped growing or that we're bound by our lies. Simply put, pride is a primary form of deception. Let's look at how this pride surfaces in the Jews in John 8:33–38, *"'But we are descendants of Abraham,' they said. 'We have never been slaves to anyone. What do you mean, 'You will be set free'?' Jesus replied, 'I tell you the truth, everyone who sins is a slave of sin. A slave is not a permanent member of the family, but a son is part of the family forever. So if the Son sets you free, you are truly free. Yes, I realize that you are descendants of Abraham. And yet some of you are trying to kill me because there's no room in your hearts for my message. I am telling you what I saw when I was with my Father. But you are following the advice of your father.'"*

Their response paraphrased, "But there's no way we are deceived because we are descendants of Abraham. We are Jews. We're immune from deception!" Translate that into today's church, and it might sound a bit like this: "But I'm a believer! I've gone to church for 30 years, so I can't be deceived!" Or "I'm not prone to deception. I'm more spiritual than you are, so I'm fine." I know a lot of Christians who believe they are not in bondage but are just as bound by lies as those who don't know Christ. 1 John 1:8 says, *"If we claim we have no sin, we are only fooling ourselves and not living in truth."* It is this ego that deceives us and keeps us from living in truth. No one is immune; pride fools us all. Ironically, assuming you aren't deceived is the biggest deception of all!

I love the Church and believe God uses the Church as His primary way of proving just how much He can do with imperfect people. I've also been deeply wounded by those imperfect people. The greatest wounds haven't come from people who unintentionally said something insensitive or from someone who failed to follow through on a commitment. Instead, the greatest wounds have come at the hands of people who were "right" and would go to any lengths to prove they were right, at my expense. I've been slandered and had lies told about me, all so a leader could attempt to prove himself to be "right" in a situation. Ironically, he was wrong. His facts were erroneous and his approach was Biblically wrong. I learned from that experience that you can't compete with the lies other people believe. You can't convince someone they are deceived or that their ego is preventing them from seeing truth. That leader was deceived about his deception, and the stronghold of pride rejected anyone who might try to speak truth. Through the grace of God, I came to a place of compassion when I realized the effects on his life were more damaging than the effects of his lies on me. I no longer wanted truth for my own defense, but truth for his freedom. His soul was held captive by the father of lies. He was bound and didn't know it.

Most of the lies we believe have been around so long that we don't realize they are lies. Lies that are familiar seem like truth. Jesus cares about truth so much that He's willing to disrupt your life so He can disrupt your lies. He's willing to offend your ego so He can deliver you from your deception. He's willing to allow your lies to fail you so you will grasp for truth. So, how can you know if you are living in deception? Here's a quick self-assessment:

- ☐ I sometimes feel unworthy, insignificant, or inadequate.
- ☐ I sometimes feel insecure, fearful, or anxious.
- ☐ I am harboring unforgiveness or resentment.
- ☐ I have a sense of exclusivity or superiority towards others.
- ☐ I sometimes feel alone or abandoned.

If you checked any of those boxes, you have deception in your life. If you didn't check any of the above, you are deceived about being deceived! We're all deceived in some way. If pride resists truth, humility invites it. The question is, Are you willing to humble yourself and give the Holy Spirit access to your heart to reveal your deception?

PRAYER POINT: *Lord, I confess deception and pride are in my heart and thought-life. I repent and ask for Your forgiveness. Holy Spirit, I ask You to reveal the pride in my heart so it can be cut away and replaced with Your Truth. I choose to humble myself, and I choose to surrender my life to Your Lordship. Teach me to walk in humility and submission. In Jesus's Name, Amen.*

Chapter 4: The Nature of Truth

⑨ Truth creates lasting transformation.

How many times have you tried to change a habit only to slide back into old patterns within a few days? Perhaps the behavior you feel stuck in is one you've attempted to overcome many times. Maybe you've read self-help books, joined accountability groups, even downloaded the newest app to help you change, only to fail again, which made you beat yourself up for not being disciplined enough, determined enough, or strong enough!

Romans 12:2 says, *"Don't copy the behavior and customs of this world, but let God transform you into a new person by changing the way you think."* As long as misconceptions, half-truths, and lies drive your behavior, you will be unable to change—no matter how hard you try. But when you come face-to-face with truth and respond to it, you will begin to see transformation take place in your life. Truth leads to change that sticks.

Jesus rebuked the Jews because there was no room in their hearts to receive the truth of His message. As the Lord begins to peel back each lie you believe, you will find not only freedom but also the space to fill your heart with truth. I think of it like this: One of my favorite suitcases for travel is a suitcase that has the expanding zipper. The expanding zipper allows you to make more room in the bag and is very handy when you end a trip with more stuff than you started. I haven't figured out why these aren't a standard issue on jeans yet, but maybe someday! We like the idea of adding Jesus to our existing suitcase (heart) full of junk by making more room. We want to expand our hearts so there's room for him among lies, sin, unforgiveness, anger, and pride. But He longs for us to unpack our hearts so He alone can fill it. Making room in our hearts isn't about adding Jesus to the junk that is there. It's about getting rid of the waste, which allows Him to fill our hearts. You might be stuck in certain behaviors because your thought-life is so filled with junk that there isn't room for truth.

10 The truth is often offensive.

Have you ever said to your child, "You're behaving like your father"? I'm guessing if you have, it wasn't a compliment and was likely describing undesirable behavior. The conversation continues in verses 39–41, *"'No,' Jesus replied, 'for if you were really the children of Abraham, you would follow his example. Instead, you are trying to kill me because I told you the truth, which I heard from God. Abraham never did such a thing. No, you are imitating your real father.'"* This seems like a harsh response from Jesus—to tell them they are children of the devil! Surely, He could have found a more palatable way to say this. His truth is offensive because it challenges our pride. We're used to being coddled with politically correct words where constructive feedback is sandwiched between compliments to soften the blow. The result is an anemic Christianity that lacks power and effectiveness. Watered-down truth lacks the power to transform.

Just as the Jews of that day wanted a politically correct Jesus with a soothing message, we long for a version of the truth that makes us feel good. But that's not the truth at all. Yes, the truth sets you free, but before the truth sets you free, it also cleanses you. It's like pouring hydrogen peroxide on a wound: It hurts, but it's good for you. Not washing the wound can allow infection that becomes much more painful in the long run.

We never see Jesus soften truth to appeal to the crowds. He never lowers the standard of truth, but instead calls people up to the standard. He won't sacrifice, compromise, or water down the truth to make you comfortable. His love won't allow Him to do those things. He wants to set you free so you can fulfill your destiny, and He'll step all over your toes to do it.

CHAPTER 5

THE NATURE OF A LIE

The clearest model of how a lie works is seen in the original lie in the Garden of Eden. The garden was a real place that serves as an ever-present promise that God will one day restore heaven on earth. In it, no one ever got stuck. There was no sickness, strife, or shame. Adam and Eve were entirely free to be exactly who God created them to be, nothing more and nothing less. They had unhindered access to God and experienced Him in His fullness. Here, truth was the perfect operating system, shaping identities, guiding human interaction, and bringing order to life.

Deep in each one of us is a longing to live and thrive in this type of environment. This is why Paul says in Hebrews 13:14, *"For this world is not our permanent home; we are looking forward to a home yet to come."* We long to live in a place where we cannot get stuck. We're hardwired to want more.

The introduction of sin into the world corrupted our operating systems. From that point on, man has been born with a sinful operating system that is prone to be deceived and inclined to get stuck. This operating system can only be restored to default through salvation and the subsequent renewing of our minds with truth.

The enemy wants to limit your life in every way, just as an outdated operating system would limit my computer's capabilities. He wants your marriage to fall short, your ministry to be subpar, your career to be lackluster, and your friendships to be ordinary. Since all lies aim to limit you, all lies have the potential to become thresholds in your life.

Consider what Paul says in Ephesians 4:22–24 (NIV), *"You were taught, with regard to your former way of life, to put off your old self, which is being corrupted by its deceitful desires; to be made new in the attitude of your minds; and to put on the new self, created to be like God in true righteousness and holiness."* Notice the correlation between a former way of life and thinking, contrasted with a renewed mind for a new way of living. He describes sinful nature as being corrupted by deception. "Corruption" means to deteriorate from one state to a lower state. "Deception" in Greek is a false impression, to be cheated or deceived by trickery and fraud. These desires lead us away from true righteousness and holiness and towards fraudulent promises, which is a deterioration of our design.

On the other hand, "renewed" means to move from one state to a higher state. In keeping with the computer illustration, you might say lies work to impair the system by infiltrating it with viruses. But the cross serves as a reset button, carrying the power to be restored to our original settings.

Let's rewind to the Book of Genesis to see the origin of deception in the world so we can better understand how Satan corrupts our thought processes with his lies. Satan's first activity in the world is the deception of Eve. Though none of us were in the garden that day, the pattern continues today. We can become skilled at identifying his work by learning the characteristics of a lie and the pattern Satan uses to form them.

Characteristics of a Lie

1. **Lies come from the enemy.**

In John 8, Jesus labels Satan as a liar, which means "one who distorts or misleads." It is his very nature to distort and mislead you. This is the essence of deception, and it's all he knows how to do. I live a truthful life, but I occasionally mess up and lie— usually a small white lie or a lie of omission to keep me out of hot water. Just because I occasionally lie does not mean my overall character or nature is to be a liar. It means I'm a mostly truthful person that messes up sometimes. Satan, on the other hand, is a liar through and through. John 8:44 says, *"He has always hated the truth, because there is no truth in him. When he lies, it is consistent with his character; for he is a liar and the father of lies."* He can't help himself. His plan has always been to kill, steal from, and destroy you, and he does it through lies. His first activity and his only activity is deception. In fact, he is incapable of telling the truth.

Genesis 3:1 describes Satan this way: *"The serpent was the shrewdest of all the animals the Lord God had made."* The Hebrew word for "shrewd" means cunning, sensible, or crafty. A cunning person is skilled at deceiving others to get what they want. They do this at the expense of their victim. What makes a cunning person so effective is that, though their work seems effortless, there is much to their strategy behind the scenes. Each step they take is a coordinated effort, drawing you further into their web of lies. Satan is a strategic swindler who is out to cheat you—at your expense.

Take note that the enemy doesn't waltz into the garden with an impressive shiny sword to wield an overt attack on humanity. No, instead, he sneaks into the garden disguised as an ordinary serpent with helpful advice, offering to help Adam and Eve make sense of their lives. He continues to disguise his deception in the same way today. He's a one-trick pony, and if we learn his trick, we won't be fooled.

② Lies question God's trustworthiness.

It's important to note how the conversation begins between Eve and the serpent because this is how we learn to identify the beginning of a lie in our minds. His strategy hasn't changed. *"Did God really say you must not eat the fruit from any of the trees in the garden?"* (Genesis 3:1). Satan initiates his temptation with the very best deceptive tool he has: a question. "Did God *really* say you can't eat from the tree? Are you *sure* that's what He said?" The strategy seems simple and innocent. The question itself is not deceptive, but the implication is. What he's really asking is, "Why would God say that? What is He keeping from you? Can you even trust Him?"

An accusation is an allegation or charge of wrongdoing. Just as a prosecutor systematically builds evidence to support his accusations, the enemy builds a case in your mind about God's motives, others' motives, and even your own motives. This is why he is called the accuser of the brethren (Revelation 12:10). Though these allegations are false, he builds a credible case by layering lie upon lie. These accusatory lies take three different forms:

1. **His accusations deny what is true about God.**

    To question someone's motives is to question their character. Satan wants us to question God's intentions towards us because then we will question His character. These lies keep us from wholeheartedly trusting God. Jeremiah 29:11 says His intention is to give us hope and a future. If we trust His intentions towards us, then we will interpret His actions through a lens of trust. But if we view His intentions with suspicion, we will interpret His actions through a lens of distrust.

God is incapable of lying. This can be hard to grasp when our situations look nothing like what God has promised. In these times, we become most susceptible to Satan's lies about God's character. It's natural, even necessary, to have questions about God's nature when you face difficult circumstances.

People asked Jesus many questions during His ministry. Some, like the Pharisees, asked Him questions because they wanted to get Him in trouble. Jesus discerned the motive behind those questions and called them fools, blind guides, a brood of vipers, hypocrites, and serpents. It's not hard to recognize that the enemy was the source of their deceptive questioning. Others asked Him questions because they wanted what He had. These people were wrestling with their faith and questioning what they believed. Jesus never rebukes them for that, because it's part of growing and discovering truth. There are times when the Holy Spirit will stir questions to push us deeper into places of surrender.

It's not the questions we have that are the problem, it is the source. Here's a really great litmus test for determining the source of your thoughts: If your thoughts accuse God or question His motives, they are from the enemy. We must aggressively reject lies in spite of what we see! If you are in a season where your reality doesn't look like God's promise, reject the lie that God doesn't care. Reject the lie that your obedience doesn't matter. Lean into God's goodness, even if it doesn't feel good. The enemy's best tactics can't change God's character, only confuse our understanding of it!

Here are some examples of how the enemy uses accusations to plant seeds of deception in our thoughts:

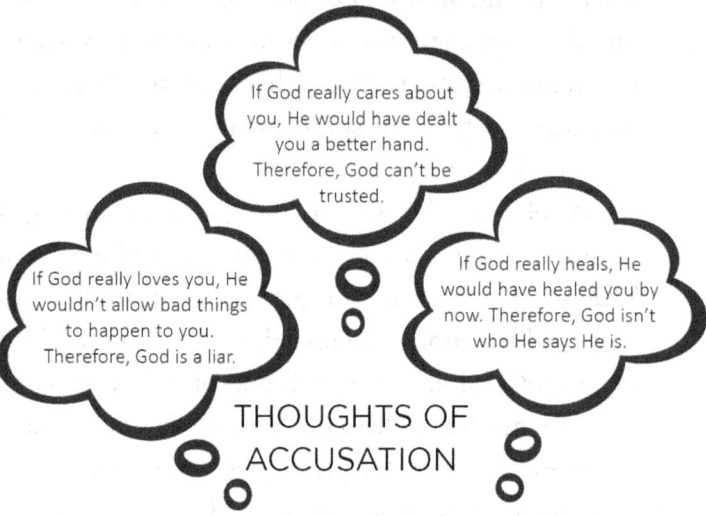

2. His accusations deny what is true about others.

One of the primary ways you can recognize the enemy's voice is that his words devalue and dishonor others. In other words, they contradict what God says about them. Judgmentalism, a critical spirit, and suspicion are forms of accusation. They cloud your ability to see others as God made them. Judgmentalism devalues others and determines what they deserve or don't deserve. A critical spirit finds fault in others, preventing us from appreciating them. Suspicion requires us to assume and assign motives. Each of these mindsets is rooted in lies. They are perversions of what God has created. Judgment is godly when we hold others to the standard God established. Criticism is healthy when it helps others grow. Discernment is a godly form of interpreting motives for the benefit of all. In their pure form, they help others. In their accusatory form, they destroy others.

These accusations aren't just to twist our perceptions of others, but to influence the way we treat them. Honor is treating people according to their God-given value. Believing the enemy's lies about others will never lead to honor.

3. **His accusations deny what is true about us.**

    His lies also contradict what God says about us. He bombards us with accusations about our sin, weaknesses, and failures. These lies bring judgment against ourselves. They tear us down and bring defeat. They twist what happens to us into a statement about who we are (or are not). They target us so we will withdraw in fear, hide in shame, or live in guilt. When we come into agreement with these lies, they become thresholds.

    The enemy repeats his accusations because he knows it adds to their credibility. Researchers have labeled this phenomenon the "illusionary truth effect." When you hear false information over and over again, you begin to believe it is true. This is the basis for slanderous political ads and the reason repeated unfounded claims about a product can convince people to buy it. Each time you hear it, it becomes a little more truthful to you. Each time you experience the same attack of the enemy, it bolsters a lie he's trying to establish in your life. We believe the repetition of an accusation makes it valid. Instead, it only reveals that the enemy repeats his behavior. A repeated accusation is a revelation of his character, not yours!

3. Lies contain an element of truth.

There's another angle to Satan's strategy in the garden that is important to see. In its most basic form, a lie is a false statement. However, a lie may also be a statement that is partially false AND partially true. The presence of truth doesn't make it less of a lie. It simply makes the lie more confusing to detect.

The enemy loves to take an element of truth and weave lies around it. Let's review how Satan does this with Eve when he questions, *"Did God really say you can't eat from all the trees in the garden?"* Notice how he starts with an "almost truth." It is true God said they couldn't eat from all the trees in the garden because God asked them to refrain from eating from one tree: the tree of the knowledge of good and evil. But the way Satan phrases it makes it sound like God was unfair by asking them to refrain. It's a subtle nuance, close enough to the truth to make it sound right, but asked in such a way that it brings real truth into question.

There are a couple of reasons this method of deception is effective. First, if he had started with an outright lie, Eve would have spotted it immediately. Had he come to Eve and said, "You know, God is mean and doesn't want you to eat the best fruit in the garden," she would have responded with, "That's not true—look at all the trees we get to eat from!" The enemy knows you are smart enough to recognize an outright lie, so he starts with the truth, almost. Second, a skilled mediator's first move is to get two disagreeing parties to agree on something trivial. The mediator will identify a point he believes both parties can easily agree upon, knowing it establishes common ground and makes subsequent agreements easier to reach. The enemy uses this very same tactic. He understands if he can get you to come into agreement with an almost truth, it makes it much easier to get you to agree with the lies that are to come.

To become skilled at identifying the lies of the enemy, we must first understand how he uses truth as a basis for his lies. For example, if I mess up, the enemy may lead with an element of truth by whispering, "You really messed up that situation." But soon that voice begins to twist the truth into a lie by saying things like, "You really are a mess up!" It's a sneaky tactic!

Eve initially answers the question with the truth of what the Lord had said. *"'Of course we may eat from the trees in the garden,' the woman replied. 'It's only the fruit from the tree in the middle of the garden that we are not allowed to eat.' God said, 'You must not eat it or even touch it; if you do, you will die'"* (Genesis 3:2–3). There appears to be no doubt in her mind about what the Lord had instructed, and we have no indication she plans to touch or eat the fruit. The enemy knows this, so he must find a more indirect way of leading her into deception. This question is a setup for what he will say next when he attacks God's promise to her.

4. Lies attack the promises God has given you.

Notice how quickly the enemy distorts the phrase "every tree but one" into "you can't eat any!" God spoke clearly to Adam and Eve about His provision. The enemy sought to rob them of the very words of the promise God spoke to them. Eve's confidence in her needs being met is eroded by the suggestion that the forbidden fruit represents an unmet need—one that God was unwilling to meet. As Eve begins to believe the lie, God's promises begin to lose their value.

One of the promises God gave Adam and Eve is the assurance they would never die—if they obeyed and did not eat from the tree. Have you ever wondered if Eve even knew what God was talking about when He said she would die if she ate of the tree? There was no death in the garden, so Eve had no experience with it. When God provides us with a promise, He always asks for our obedience without giving us the full picture. That's why faith is the evidence of things not yet experienced or seen (Hebrews 11:1). The enemy will come after the promises you don't understand to establish doubt. *"'You won't die!' the serpent replied to the woman. 'God knows that your eyes will be opened as soon as you eat it, and you will be like God, knowing both good and evil'"* (Genesis 3:4–5). He's essentially saying, "God's promise to you is a lie, so your obedience doesn't matter."

The greatest areas of promise in your life will face the most intense levels of attack. The fruit of the garden was God's very best for Eve. It was a promise of provision where she would never have to worry about what to eat. It was a promise of companionship where she would never have to worry about being lonely. It was a promise of health where she would never have to worry about being sick. And it was a promise full of God's purpose for their lives where they would never have to worry about whether they matter. The enemy's lies sought to rob her of these promises. Like a sweater with a snag, the enemy uses his lies to unravel our confidence in God's promises and provision.

5. Lies gain power from our agreement.

We see what happens next in Genesis 3:6, *"The woman was convinced. She saw that the tree was beautiful and its fruit looked delicious, and she wanted the wisdom it would give her. So she took the fruit and ate it. Then she gave some to her husband who was with her, and he ate it, too.*" The word "convinced" means that she agreed with her own thoughts. We know those thoughts were planted by the serpent and were not the product of her original operating system. Her thought processes came into agreement with what the enemy was saying. The enemy has little power over your life until your thoughts come into agreement with his. Agreement gives power to his lies.

Agreement is a Kingdom idea that the devil ripped off and twisted for his purposes. Jesus speaks of the power of agreement resulting in answered prayers in Matthew 18:19, *"I also tell you this: If two of you agree here on earth concerning anything you ask, my Father in heaven will do it for you."* The Greek word for "agree" has the same root word as "symphony" and means in harmony or like-minded. When we agree with a lie, we become like-minded with the enemy. When we agree with the Truth, we become like-minded with Christ. Our agreement becomes alignment.

Notice as soon as Eve is convinced, she begins to see differently. She suddenly sees that the tree is beautiful and the fruit looks delicious. The tree remained unchanged, but her perspective is now shaped by the lie that God was withholding from her. Without an agreement, the serpent's words were empty. With her agreement, the words became the driving force behind Eve's disobedience. What you agree with shapes what you see. What you see shapes what you do. What you do shapes the results you experience.

6. Lies skew how we experience life.

2 Corinthians 10:5 (NASB) says, "*We are destroying speculations and every lofty thing raised up against the knowledge*

of God, and we are taking every thought captive to the obedience of Christ." The enemy loves to place suggestions, assumptions, and speculations in our minds. He loves to paint a picture that doesn't exist. When we come into agreement with his suggestion, it becomes part of our thinking. When we come into agreement with an assumption, it becomes our filter of interpretation. When we come into agreement with his speculation, it jades our version of reality.

Lies affect how we interpret what happens to us. The enemy loves to challenge truth with his version of events, just as a sports commentator gives you the play-by-play of a game to help you understand what is happening. He skews your perspective so he can influence your thoughts, emotions, and behaviors. He wants you to question God's goodness, fairness, and faithfulness. The serpent's commentary about God's nature surfaces new emotions—emotions Eve had never felt. For the first time, she felt insecure and even unloved. In response to these emotions, she disobeys.

The biggest threat to the enemy's plan for your life is for you to know, with clarity, God's nature. In Adam and Eve's case, their interpretation was that God was withholding from them and that God didn't love them. For every lie you believe, there is something extraordinary about God's nature you are not seeing and trusting. Here are some common ways lies confuse us about God's nature, resulting in getting stuck:

- We wish we had someone else's talents, so we fail to understand God's heart for equipping and empowering us.
- We dwell on past rejection, so we do not experience how deeply God loves us.

- We worry about finances, so we do not understand God's provisional nature. We believe He withholds with closed fists, instead of providing with open hands.

⑦ Lies invite you into a place of self-sufficiency.

The garden represents total dependence upon God. Adam and Eve lived with complete confidence their needs would be met and that God would come through for them. There was no worry and no striving, only an abundance of peace that came from total dependency upon God.

Deception leads us away from surrender and into self-sufficiency. Self-sufficiency is the state where we rely on ourselves to meet our needs. Our un-surrendered ego (pride) loves the idea that we can meet our own needs without relying on others, and especially without relying on God. In Eve's case, if she could obtain the knowledge of the tree of good and evil, she wouldn't need to rely on God for it. The enemy appeals to her ego, which lures her into self-sufficiency. He does the same for us. Self-sufficiency is a lie, and we must aggressively deny it a place in our lives.

We cannot simultaneously choose to trust God and choose to be self-sufficient. This is why faith requires we die to ourselves each day. In doing so, we die to our "right" to be self-sufficient and choose dependence upon God. There is no other path to true peace. Even worry is the ego's way of trying to figure out or control a situation and is a form of self-sufficiency!

Here are three temptations of self-sufficiency in Eve's conversation that Satan still uses today:

1. He appeals to our desire for justice.

He appeals to her ego's desire for justice by questioning why a "good" God would withhold something "good" from her. He argued it was an injustice that God might withhold something good from her, but left out that God would only withhold something for her benefit. It is not our desire for justice that gets us in trouble; it is our thinking about what is fair and just.

2. **He appeals to our desire to be in control.**
   The serpent offers Eve the ability to take control of her own life. He says, in essence, "If you eat of this tree, you will be like God and no longer need God." This is yet another example of how Satan takes a godly principle and twists it for his destructive purposes. Surrender is godly and it makes us like God. Self-sufficiency is sin and makes us want to be God. Our desire for knowledge or understanding is a desire to gain control over a situation. He entices our egos by convincing us we can figure situations out on our own, which gives us a false sense of control. For example, if I can "diagnose" another person's motives, it gives me a sense of power in determining when and how they can hurt me in the future. If I can rehash a situation until I understand what happened to me, I feel a sense of control over the pain I feel. If I can find a way to meet my own needs, I can control my fear of lack.

3. **He appeals to our desire for more.**
   In the midst of a bountiful garden of fruitful trees, he appeals to her ego's desire for security with the lure of more. Eve had everything she needed, and yet it didn't feel like enough. He appeals to our ego by creating a scarcity mentality, which is a fear that God won't provide.

It is the belief there will be enough for others, but not enough for me. It is a lie. The enemy has a way of making our lives look like they aren't enough—and to convince us to take it upon ourselves to make them enough.

Forms of self-sufficiency, such as addiction (meeting needs with our effort) and religion (trying to measure up with our effort) move us away from God. The Israelites wandered in circles in the wilderness because they refused to trust God. It was the lie of self-sufficiency that had them stuck in the wilderness. And yet, God used that 40-year season to bring them back to find their source in Him. You see, God allows us to go through situations where our efforts fail us so we can learn to find sufficiency in Him. With our back to the wall, He exposes the lies our ego is so prone to believe that might prevent us from seeing our need for Him. Here's what God had to say to the Israelites about this process in Deuteronomy 8:2–3, "*Remember how the LORD your God led you through the wilderness for these forty years, humbling you and testing you to prove your character, and to find out whether or not you would obey his commands. Yes, he humbled you by letting you go hungry and then feeding you with manna, a food previously unknown to you and your ancestors. He did it to teach you that people do not live by bread alone; rather, we live by every word that comes from the mouth of the LORD.*"

As you walk through the process of becoming unstuck, the Holy Spirit will surface the lies you believe and invite you into a place of surrender. Surrender is a key component of becoming unstuck—it is the shortest path to experiencing the peace and provision promised for believers. We were not made to live on bread alone (what man can produce), but instead to be sustained by the truth that comes from God.

⑧ Lies promise an easier way.

I enjoy fishing. Depending upon the type of fish I want to catch, I use various types of lures and bait. A good fisherman (or fisherwoman) knows you can't catch a fish with just a hook because the hook itself has no appeal to the fish. Instead, you conceal the purpose of the hook with bait to trick the fish into biting. Bait makes it look innocent, even tasty. In the same way, Satan baits us with an "easier" way to meet our needs than trusting God.

Eve liked the sound of what the serpent was saying because it offered an easy way into what she wanted. Another definition for the Hebrew "shrewd" is sensible. The enemy brings a lie to you that sounds sensible, reasonable, and logical. This is what makes his lies so difficult to recognize and dismantle. He made it all sound so easy—all you have to do is eat, and you will have all the knowledge you've ever wanted. It's like the diet commercial that says, "All you have to do is take this pill, and you'll lose weight." Most things that start with "all you have to do…" are scams. We believe lies because they offer us something. They tell us what we want to hear, and never what we need to hear. If they didn't, we wouldn't fall for them!

In addition to making it easy, the enemy's distortion offered immediate gratification—eat, and you will know *as soon as you eat it*. In other words, eat, and you will be like God…now. This is the same temptation that tricks a fish into biting a lure before realizing the danger. The enemy's lies offer an immediate payoff but carry a long-term cost. They are a bait and switch.

We love the idea of "now," but unfortunately, most of God's promises don't include "now" as a descriptor! God's command to Adam and Eve was "don't eat" (short-term cost) and the promise was "you will live" (long-term reward). The promises of God for

Chapter 5: The Nature of a Lie

your life are long-term; they carry eternal weight. Things of that magnitude won't come easy and they won't come fast.

We often equate spiritual maturity with the amount of Scriptural knowledge a person has acquired or the longevity of someone's walk with the Lord. But Paul defines maturity as denying lies a place in our lives in exchange for God's long-term plan. Ephesians 4:14 says, *"Then we will no longer be immature like children. We won't be tossed and blown about by every wind of new teaching. We will not be influenced when people try to trick us with lies so clever they sound like the truth."* A child will give in to what they want at the moment because they have not developed the self-control necessary for delayed gratification. Childish thinking is prone to believe lies, especially when they sound like the truth. Spiritual maturity is recognizing the convenience of a lie and choosing truth anyway.

⑨ Lies are an attack on your God-given identity.

Every attack of the enemy on your life is an attack on your identity. Each lie is crafted to keep you from walking in the freedom of who God designed you to be. Remember the iceberg illustration where we talked about the power of what lies below the surface to influence what you see above? Our identity is usually associated with things you can see, like personalities, talents, careers, ministries, and relationships—but these things are all byproducts of our thinking below the surface.

We can all, by design, have a secure identity hidden within the unshakable, unmovable identity of God. A skyscraper's strength comes from pylons that extend far beneath the surface into the bedrock. Not only do these pylon foundations support the weight of the building, but they also keep it anchored in strong winds and act as a stabilizer in small earthquakes. When we connect our identity to His, it is more than enough to support the weight of our lives and the adversity we face. An unshakeable identity is found in Him.

Our issue of identity and every lie of the enemy always comes back to this central question: Is God truly who He says He is? If the answer is yes, then I am who He says I am—and we cannot believe He is enough while believing we are not enough. If the answer is no, then I cannot trust what God says about my identity, either.

Consider how a fun house mirror at an amusement park distorts your image. When you look into the mirror, you recognize your image (an element of truth), but the mirror reflects your image in a distorted manner. This is the same way the enemy presents to you a distorted, inaccurate version of who you are.

> ### **Rebecca's Story: Stuck in Perfectionism**
>
> A dear friend of mine is gorgeous, athletic, witty, talented, anointed, loves the Lord, and deeply desires to live a life pleasing to Him. Rebecca has everything going for her, and yet, for many years she believed the enemy's reflection of who she was. What she believed about herself was the exact opposite of God's truth. She grew up in the church, went to Christian school, and knows the Word—which shows that no one is immune from deception.
>
> The fear of rejection and of her inadequacies being exposed paralyzed her for years. She chose to shrink back from ministry, opportunities, and relationships instead of stepping into them. Remaining invisible was safer than being seen and known. She couldn't afford to take the risk that others might see the ugliness and

> inadequacies she saw—all lies. For the areas of her life people could see, she pursued perfectionism at the expense of peace, relationships, and purpose.
>
> I was privileged to have a front-row seat to the deep work God did in Rebecca's life to uproot those lies. One by one, He addressed them by healing past hurts and revealing His truth in those places. As He did, that distorted reflection became less and less twisted, and she began to step out into her true identity. One of many great outcomes was that she stepped into her calling as a worship leader. She now leads with boldness and confidence in her talents, anointing, and most importantly, in who she is as a child of God. When she sings from that place of freedom, God uses her to set other people free. Rebecca wreaks havoc on hell, so it's no wonder the attack of lies has been so strategic and fierce. The enemy attacked her identity because it was worth his attention. Yours is, too.

⑩ Lies are destructive to our lives.

As soon as Adam and Eve bought into the lie and ate the fruit, it altered their operating systems. The serpent had promised they would understand good and evil, but the outcome wasn't what they expected. Though the fruit promised she would attain equality with God, it was an empty promise. A lie always promises an elevated state but delivers the opposite result. For example, the lie of greed promises importance, happiness, and security but instead produces fear, insecurity, and loneliness. The lie of unforgiveness promises to protect us from pain and punish the offender but instead traps us in pain and punishes us. A lie never delivers on its promise. (Good news—the truth always does!)

Instead, the lie produced a destructive chain reaction of shame, fear, and division. These three things continue to get us stuck today.

Shame

The first result of sin was that Adam and Eve realized they were naked. Before this, shame did not exist, and they had nothing to hide. The origin of the word "shame" means to cover or hide. If you cover something, you put something over an object to protect or conceal it. If you hide something, you put it out of sight so it isn't noticed. Shame does just that—it's a lie that makes us want to hide who we truly are and present a version of ourselves we think others will like. Even though this is our sinful nature, it goes against our design. We are created to be vulnerable with one another and with God. It is unnatural for us to be guarded, protect ourselves, or be defensive. If you're going against your nature, it's exhausting. Think about a difficult conversation you've had where both you and the other person have been open and vulnerable. These conversations are almost effortless. Or think about a time when you got something off your chest, and you felt relieved. That's because God created us to be vulnerable.

Their nakedness had been pure and innocent, but their new knowledge (way of thinking) caused them to feel ashamed and exposed. The lie they believed about God, that He can't be trusted, permeated their thoughts about everything else. They couldn't trust each other's motives or thoughts, so they sewed fig leaves together to protect themselves. The transparency of their relationship was gone, and in its place were barriers to intimacy.

After they covered themselves to hide from one another, they still felt the need to hide from God (Genesis 3:8). This kind of hiding means to draw back or to conceal. For the first time, they felt self-conscious, inadequate, and were afraid of God's presence. So, they withdrew and hid.

> **Aaron's Story: Stuck in Shame**
>
> Aaron had a call to ministry and had filled many roles within the church for years. Unfortunately, he had also experienced disappointment, betrayal, and repeated failure. Because he had been trained in weak theology that downplays the importance of facing pain, those wounds festered and grew. When they would start to affect his ability to minister at one church, he would leave for a new ministry opportunity elsewhere. His pain and unhealthy patterns followed him.
>
> After years of this, the past hurts and failures cultivated a distrust in God and others. He resented God for his calling and was bitter that the church had failed him. Underneath, he hated himself for being a failure.
>
> When his patterns caught up with him one last time, he collapsed under the weight of his shame and gave in to deception. He adopted a paranoid mindset and believed it was him against the world. Rather than surfacing these lies and facing his pain, he blamed everyone else and lashed out at anyone who might speak truth. He sought to control everyone around him in an attempt to keep his pain from controlling him. As he spiraled further into these self-destructive behaviors, he left a wake of carnage in his path, leaving many confused and wounded themselves.
>
> It wasn't long before he cut off all outside relationships and began controlling those inside his home. It cost him his ministry, his friendships, the respect of his children, and the health of his marriage. Most

> tragically, he distanced himself from any relationship with God and swore off any future ministry. Though Aaron had an opportunity to deal with his shame, he chose to withdraw and hide.

There was an element of truth in Aaron's pain and an element of truth to Adam and Eve's nakedness. It wasn't the truth that caused them to hide, but instead their errant thinking about the truth.

God watches all of this unfold with Adam and Eve. He watches Eve eat the fruit and then hand it to her husband, then watches them scramble to cover themselves with leaves. Finally, He watches them hide from Him—and yet He still comes to seek them out. The same is true for you and me. He never retreats, even when we do. He never turns away in disgust, even when we sin. Instead, He comes calling for us. Like the shepherd that leaves the 99 sheep to find the one lost sheep, He comes after us in our deceived state to draw us back into relationship.

Not only did God come to find them in the garden, but He calls out to Adam, *"Where are you?"* (Genesis 3:9). God knew exactly where they were. So why did He ask this question? It is profound that God's first question to Adam and Eve after they sinned wasn't, "What did you do?" or "Why did you do that?" Rather, it was, "Where are you?" The first question would have focused on their behavior and the second would have shamed them for messing up. But God's question focused on relationship. They felt unworthy; He wanted them to know they were worth finding. They felt unlovable; He wanted them to know His love would pursue them. They felt the need to hide; He wanted to be where they were. They believed lies, but He was bringing them truth.

With this question, Adam and Eve have a choice. They can continue to hide, or they can return to a loving Father. The cross is this same invitation to us. This invitation goes beyond the initial point of salvation and extends to any place in our lives where we have distanced ourselves from Him. In His grace, He calls out to us in our deceived state and invites us to find our way back home. When Adam responds, it begins his journey from deception back to truth. Adam's response has nothing to do with his location and everything to do with the condition of his heart.

Fear

A close friend of shame is fear. Fear doesn't exist in the garden until this point. Adam replies, *"I heard you walking in the garden, so I hid. I was afraid because I was naked"* (Genesis 3:10). Adam was created to walk and talk with God, and it is through this uninhibited relationship that he gets his needs met. Now that he's afraid and aware of his nakedness, he hides from the very relationship that represents his full potential. Fear causes us to live at a lesser level and hide from the very things that are designed to bring out the greatness in us. Fear will cause us to compromise our standards, choose what is easy instead of what is right, and stay in a place that is far below God's best.

For the first time in his life, Adam lost his peace. Since we have peace when our thoughts are aligned with truth, it only makes sense that thoughts based on lies breed fear. Remember, our emotions follow our thoughts.

There is a counterfeit version of peace that gets and keeps us stuck. This pseudo-peace is the absence of conflict or friction. We may stay stuck in an unhealthy relationship cycle for the sake of feeling comfortable—at the expense of experiencing true peace. We may stay in a job because we like the "peace" that comes with familiarity and predictability—at the expense of having a job that aligns with our values and purpose. What feels like peace is actually a form of fear.

Here's a hard-hitting truth—no one can take genuine peace from you because peace comes from alignment with the Father. Note in verse 10 that Adam wasn't afraid of God. Why? God's nature hadn't changed. Instead, he was afraid because he realized he was naked. Something had changed in his thinking. He moved away from truth, and in the process, moved away from peace and moved away from the Lord. Isaiah 26:3 says, *"You will keep in perfect peace all who trust in you, all whose thoughts are fixed on you."* God's peace never moves away from us, we move away from it. Even the worst situation can't move us away from the perfect peace that comes from the Father.

The process of getting unstuck will undoubtedly lead you into places where your pseudo-peace gets rocked. You will be tempted by fear to return to the status quo because it's easier and feels safer. When you cross your threshold, you move towards peace—a peace that surpasses understanding and that guards your heart and your mind (Philippians 4:7).

Division

The introduction of sin in the garden was also the introduction of division into Adam and Eve's relationship. The power of unity goes both ways. Whatever you choose to unite yourself with will yield powerful results in your life. Godly unity shakes the kingdom of hell. But Adam and Eve had ungodly unity because they sinned in unity. They came into unity and agreement with the lie, together.

Their division becomes evident when they begin placing blame for their actions. The Lord asks them if they have eaten

Chapter 5: The Nature of a Lie

from the tree, and they start to point fingers. His question isn't to make them feel guilty. It's to allow them to take ownership. In the Kingdom of God, the restoration of a relationship always begins with ownership. We become restored in relationship to God when we take ownership of our need for a Savior. We become restored in relationship to others when we take ownership of our behavior and its impacts. Personal ownership is the foundation of a mutual relationship.

But since Adam and Eve now believe the lie that they can't trust God or one another, neither takes ownership, but instead, they try to protect themselves. The man replied, *"It was the woman you gave me who gave me the fruit, and I ate it"* (Genesis 3:12). Without a doubt, Adam is responsible for his actions. He chose the woman over obedience. Was it that he overheard the conversation with the serpent and was himself deceived? Or was he worried about losing his place in the garden and didn't want to be overshadowed by Eve's newfound knowledge? Or was Adam just that gullible? Regardless, he's responsible and accountable for the choice he made. When God asks Adam about his behavior, note what he says: *"It was the woman you gave me…"* (emphasis mine). Not only was it Eve's fault, but it was God's fault because He gave Eve to Adam! Then God turns to Eve and asks her the same question, and she blames the serpent God created. It was God's fault again!

Blame will always get you stuck. It distances you from personal accountability and makes someone else responsible. In the process, it distances us from others. Blame represents a breach of relationship and trust. It takes away our responsibility, and along with it, the opportunity to make things better. Blame will never help you cross a threshold but accepting healthy responsibility will.

Disobedience

As we previously discussed, transformation doesn't happen through sheer self-discipline or avoidance of certain behaviors. True change happens when we allow the Holy Spirit to replace the lies we believe with the truth systematically. Religion has wrongly convinced people that if they just try harder, have more self-discipline, avoid temptation, or pray more that their life will improve. These things can be helpful, but they only treat the symptoms if we don't allow the Holy Spirit to go below the surface.

Obedience is an extension of identity. When Eve's identity is found in a relationship with her Father, obedience is natural. This makes rebellion (disobedience) an issue of a faulty identity. When we believe God's truth, we have no desire to sin. Romans 1:25 says, *"They traded the truth about God for a lie. So they worshipped and served the things God created instead of the Creator himself..."* The believers in Rome had faulty beliefs, so their worship was misplaced. Your beliefs shape your allegiance, and your allegiance shapes your obedience.

The enemy's number one goal isn't to destroy your job, finances, health, marriage, or ministry. He is after your obedience most of all because disobedience gives him legal ground to kill, steal, and destroy.

Chapter 5: The Nature of a Lie

Construction of a Lie

Here's a visual summary of how the enemy constructs a lie:

CONSTRUCTION OF A LIE

STEP 1 — START WITH TRUTH
BEGIN WITH AN ELEMENT OF TRUTH
Did God really say, "Don't eat from the tree?"

STEP 2 — DISTORT THE TRUTH
DISTORT THAT ELEMENT OF TRUTH
God doesn't want you to eat; He is withholding from you.

STEP 3 — PLANT THE LIE
USE THE DISTORTION TO PLANT A LIE
God is withholding; He must not want what is best for you.

STEP 4 — GAIN AGREEMENT
GAIN AGREEMENT WITH THE LIE
God doesn't want what is best for you; He cannot be trusted.

STEP 5 — ESTABLISH A STRONGHOLD
AGREEMENT ESTABLISHES A STRONGHOLD
God cannot be trusted; I must be self-sufficient.

STEP 6 — PRODUCE RESULTS
DISOBEDIENCE BRINGS ABOUT DESTRUCTION
I am self-sufficient so I live separate from God.

Each step builds upon the last until it becomes embedded in your life. You can see how the compounding effects of many subtle deceptions gain power and influence, leading to destruction. If you believe a lie about yourself or your circumstances, don't beat yourself up—it's the oldest trick in the Book (literally). The best news about realizing you believe a lie is knowing that your Heavenly Father longs to reveal Himself to you in the place of that lie. He never roots out a lie without providing truth to fill the gap. What has been constructed can also be deconstructed, restored, and redeemed.

CHAPTER 6

HOW WE GET TRAPPED IN OUR THOUGHTS

To summarize so far, a threshold is a lie we believe that limits us in some way. We've learned how Satan plants lies, so now it's time to learn how those lies become thresholds. These lies "trap" us in a certain way of thinking, feeling, and behaving. In Biblical terms, this is called a stronghold.

Thought traps become strongholds.

Patterns in our lives are connected to a correlating pattern of thinking. A singular thought may influence behavior, but patterns of thought influence patterns of behavior. When we come into agreement with destructive patterns of thinking, our lives align with those patterns. This is a stronghold.

Proverbs 26:11 says, "*As a dog returns to its vomit, so a fool repeats his foolishness.*" This is a strange verse, and I wonder if God included it just to get our attention. As a proud dog owner, I have witnessed this repulsive behavior on more than one occasion. Though dogs are smart animals, they have some habits and behaviors that seem ridiculous (and gross) by human standards. Ironically, a dog returns to lick up its vomit, even though there was something that caused their body to reject it. They are attracted to the very thing that made them sick and compelled to repeat their behavior. From an outsider's perspective, it's easy to see that returning is a poor choice, and yet it makes complete sense to the dog!

Why are we compelled to repeat our mistakes and return to the very things that cause us pain and heartache? It turns out we might not be all that different than the dog Solomon referenced in Proverbs. A dog has faulty thinking and isn't able to understand why returning to their vomit may be harmful to them. In the same way, we repeat harmful behaviors because of our faulty thinking.

In Scripture, a stronghold is a false argument in which someone seeks shelter or a safe place to escape reality. It is a way of thinking that begins as a form of protection, like a fortress with walls, but soon becomes a prison that locks us into certain behaviors and patterns. It is a lie that is so embedded in your thinking that it has become part of your identity and filters what you experience.

That lie has a "strong-hold" on you, which makes it nearly impossible to break free from your cycle. It is something we can't get free from, no matter how hard we try or how strong our willpower is. This is because our deep-seated beliefs, under the surface, trump what we know. These types of stronghold beliefs guide our lives in the way a rudder steers a ship from under the surface.

Here are some examples of stronghold beliefs:
- We know overeating is unhealthy, but deep beliefs about our self-worth subvert our logic.
- We recognize a toxic relationship, but our fear of rejection convinces us to stay.
- We know we should save money, but we are addicted to the adrenaline of buying something new.
- We know we should be more confident, but our shame keeps us stuck in insecurity.
- We know we should forgive, but we aren't willing to give up the feeling of control we gain from our anger.

Reflection question: What is something you know you should do (or shouldn't do), but you continue to do it anyway? What lie is behind that stronghold?

Thought Trap

I've previously illustrated a thought process as a linear process for the sake of simplicity. However, a cycle is a more accurate picture of how a stronghold thought process works in our lives. When it comes to cyclical behaviors, we must begin to see our thoughts as cyclical processes.

Psychologists use a concept called "thought loops" to describe this cycle, but it doesn't capture the role of lies in the sequence. Without identifying the lie, the best we can do is will ourselves to think differently rather than being set free from old ways of thinking! The secular version offers information but no hope or true path to transformation. I've created a version that shows the progression of a lie in a cyclical model and how it impacts our behavior. These are the same six steps outlined in "The Construction of a Lie" illustration in the previous chapter.

THE FORMATION OF A THOUGHT TRAP

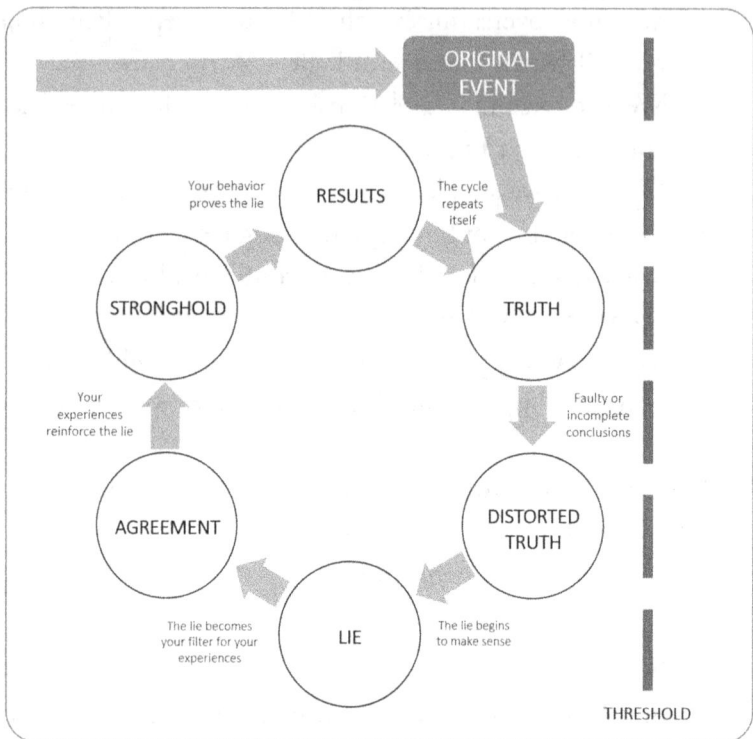

When I was young, going to the mall was a big deal. It wasn't just the stores and the food court that were fun but all of the activities in the mall corridor. One of these activities was a spiral wishing well. These wells allow you to donate a coin to a worthy cause in a fun way. You drop a coin in the slot and it begins to spin around the vortex, with gravity pulling it faster and faster towards the opening at the bottom of the funnel. I can still hear the sound of the coin looping over and over again and picking up speed with each pass.

This spiral is what happens with our thought cycles. As we repeat the cycle, it picks up momentum, feeds itself, and begins to drive our lives. The only way to stop the cycle is to disrupt it. I can stop the coin from going in the opening of the funnel by reaching down and grabbing it. We disrupt our thought traps when we reach down and "grab the thought." This is why Paul tells us to capture every rebellious thought and teach them to obey Christ (2 Corinthians 10:5). To capture means to bring under control rather than be controlled by. Paul knew these lies have the potential to become a trap.

> ### Elizabeth's Story: Stuck in Shame
>
> A teacher called on Elizabeth to answer a math problem when she was in third grade. When put on the spot, Elizabeth stumbled over her words and gave an incorrect answer. In response, the teacher scolded her and called her an idiot in front of the class. To add insult to injury, the teacher then threw an eraser at her. Her classmates laughed and she was utterly humiliated.
>
> At that moment, eight-year-old Elizabeth could not process the pain of what had happened. A child's limited reasoning interprets what happens to him or her based on what they know and have experienced. Since Elizabeth knew an authority figure should not treat a child like that, her brain (assisted by a suggestion from the enemy) concluded there must be something wrong with her to deserve that kind of extreme response. Elizabeth decided that day that she was worth rejecting because she wasn't smart.
>
> The lie progressed when Elizabeth subconsciously agreed that she would avoid similar painful experiences in the future by dodging any situation that might expose her as "not being smart enough." Instead, she would earn people's approval by being the prettiest in the room and the life of the party. Though she is

> naturally beautiful and has a fun personality, her new identity shielded her from situations where she would need to use her brain. In the process, these mechanisms insulated her from experiencing the pain of third-grade math class again. Unfortunately, it also required Elizabeth to build a life where her looks and personality defined her identity, friendships, and career. Though the painful classroom experience was years behind her, this unhealed wound was, in fact, steering her life. Eventually, these mechanisms that once served her well by helping her avoid pain became thresholds. The things that defined her identity, friendships, and career started to limit those very areas of her life.
>
> As Elizabeth began to receive healing, her thoughts gradually began to change. It didn't happen overnight, but slowly over time, lies were replaced with truth. As she started to live out the truth, she found new confidence and freedom—and discovered she was actually quite smart.

Many times, you will find your threshold served a helpful purpose in the beginning. Over time, the lie of inadequacy had become a stronghold, steering Elizabeth away from opportunities and into destructive cycles. The spiral had momentum in her life, and she didn't know how to get free.

Wherever there is a destructive pattern or cycle, there is a lie buried beneath the surface. Elizabeth bought into the lie that she wasn't good enough (shame). Because she believed this, she determined there was something inherently wrong with the way she was created, and she would have to become someone else in order to be loved and accepted. This pretense was a way of

Chapter 6: How We Get Trapped in Our Thoughts

hiding that helped her control the pain of feeling inadequate. Simultaneously, it created a deep internal conflict that spiraled her even further into the stronghold.

In addition, it perpetuated the lie, creating a vicious cycle. Since she avoided situations that might make her feel dumb, this only reinforced her belief and others' perceptions that she was, in fact, not smart. The cycle repeated itself with these self-fulfilling prophecies until she was finally able to disrupt her thinking. Let's see how Elizabeth's thought trap played out:

ELIZABETH'S THOUGHT TRAP

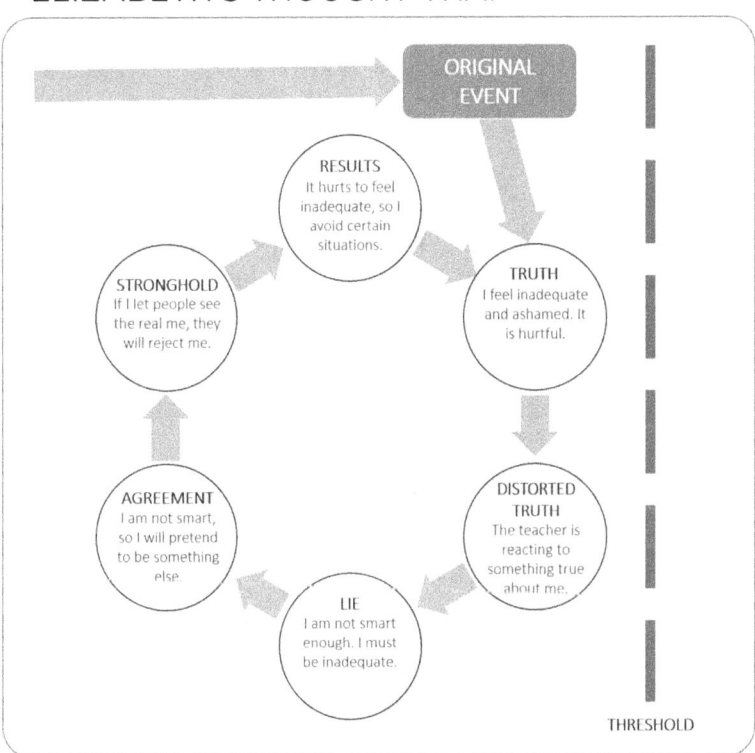

Until a new way of thinking disrupted the thought trap, Elizabeth would experience the same emotions, behaviors, and results. She could not change the cruel circumstance that set the initial cycle into motion, but she could receive emotional healing so the original event was no longer a threshold. Since the lie was attached to the event, she had to detach from the painful experience. God's design for healing is to bring the truth of His love into that wounded place until it is made whole.

Thought Traps Start with an Event

Our beliefs come from the events that shape the way we define and experience our lives. As was true for Elizabeth, a lie begins with an event, usually one in which we experience a deep hurt or disappointment. These incidents may be a painful argument, an accident, or an offense. It might be a sin you committed (within your control) or a wrong committed against you (outside of your control).

There are several reasons the enemy uses painful events to introduce lies into our thinking. First, when we are hurting, it affects how we process our world and skews the conclusions we draw from our experiences. Since our brains want to make sense of what is happening, we are eager to latch on to the first idea that brings resolution. When Elizabeth felt embarrassed and rejected, the enemy took advantage of her vulnerability and flooded her thought-life with lies about her worth.

Very often, our lies have their origin in childhood events. Like Elizabeth, children have an undeveloped ability to interpret what happens to them. They lack the experience, context, and maturity needed to draw accurate conclusions about their experiences. As a result, they are prone to believe how others treat them is related to their worth.

As we move into adulthood, the enemy plants his greatest lies when you are in difficult seasons. He knows that's when you are

Chapter 6: How We Get Trapped in Our Thoughts

weakest and most prone to deception. It's in the hard seasons that feel very unfair, and when you are feeling self-pity that the enemy launches his most intense attacks—and when we are least likely to recognize them. The deepest lies we believe about ourselves and others were planted in the soil of hurt, loneliness, and confusion.

If you want to identify the source of what you believe, ask the Holy Spirit to reveal the event or series of events that caused the wound. If you don't feel beautiful, maybe it's because someone made fun of you at a young age. If you don't feel worthy, perhaps it's because your mother disapproved of you. If you feel like a failure, maybe it's because you've experienced the humiliation of failing. When He reveals the event, He will also expose the lie and heal the hurt.

Second, the event itself shelters the lie. Because there is an element of truth in what happened to you, it protects the lie you believe. Remember, the enemy loves to take the truth and distort it. In short, he disguises lies underneath the cloak of actual events and adds his commentary to help you "understand" what happened to you and why. We often protect what we believe because it validates our wounds and justifies our behavior.

I once had a friend who was stuck in rejection. She had been divorced for many years and bought into the lie that she deserved rejection. Over time, that belief became a form of protection to keep her at arm's length from further pain. Her divorce was long over, but the pain of the event was still protecting her.

Next, events become part of our identity. The event becomes part of our "truth" for how we see the world and how we see ourselves within that world. We use positive milestones, like graduations, promotions, and weddings, as definition points in our lives. The enemy wants to use hurtful events to shape your identity, as well. We all know someone who is stuck in the past because they haven't gotten over something that happened. The negative event has become a defining point for their lives.

I have a former co-worker whose husband passed away several years ago of a heart attack. She was left behind to pick up the pieces and raise two young children. It was a traumatic event that altered who she was, and rightfully so. I don't want to belittle her grief or make judgments about her healing process, as I've never been in her shoes. I began to notice this topic would come up in every conversation we had. The wounds were still fresh, as though it had happened yesterday. I had compassion for her sadness, but I could see that she was mad at her husband for leaving and mad at God for taking him. It was her anger, not her grief, that tethered her to that moment when he died, preventing her from finding any peace or closure. Her anger was a stronghold steering her life and a threshold keeping her from moving on. She had abandoned her true identity for that of a grieving widow.

Lies stemming from painful events get grafted into our identity over time. I failed, so I'm a failure. I didn't get chosen, so I'm not good enough. My husband left me, so I am undesirable. These thought traps keep us bound to past events, preventing us from experiencing the present and the future.

The pain of the experience is so great that we stuff it down because we don't know how else to manage the pain. And in the process of stuffing it down, we bury the lie so deep it becomes part of our identity. Like two trees whose roots become intertwined deep in the ground, the lie becomes intertwined in who we are.

Stuck in Thought Traps

Three tactics that keep us stuck in thought traps are rumination, confirmation bias, and unresolved anger. Each of these allows past events to continue their control over our lives. Let's dive into each of these strategies.

① Rumination

One of the ways we get stuck in a thought trap is by dwelling on a situation. While the Gospel creates a natural path for us to process, release, and heal our pain to move forward, the enemy wants us to get stuck in what happened to us. I tend to replay what happened when I'm striving to make sense of it. I review over and over again, hoping to find the missing link that might help me understand and relieve my pain. But when we rehearse a situation over and over again in our minds, it becomes slightly distorted each time. These common distortions occur:

The event becomes disproportionate to reality.

Sometimes, the event becomes magnified. Have you ever noticed the more you think about what someone has done to you, the more personal the offense becomes and the angrier you feel? As we replay, we add inflection to words, exaggerate what was said or done, assign intent to behavior, and fill in gaps in conversations by attributing words to others that were never spoken. It's easy to lose sight of what actually happened!

Other times, the event becomes minimized in our recollection. We explain away or justify what happened—even making excuses for what others have done. Minimizing our experience is easier than allowing ourselves to feel the extent of the pain we feel. By diminishing it, we wrongly believe we can mitigate its effects on our lives. Instead, we bury the pain. In the way a splinter embedded in skin finds a way out, our pain comes out sideways. Buried pain from past events may get directed at people who had nothing to do with it, like your spouse, children, or even yourself. Pain doesn't go away when you bury it; it just finds a new way to express itself.

The event becomes more and more personal.

Our minds strive to make sense of what happens to us, and the enemy is eager to assist. We like clear cause and effect relationships so we can identify why something has happened. Instead of it being something that happens to us, it becomes something that happens about us.

We *should* examine the things that happen to us to determine our part so we can repent and own it. This is an opportunity for the truth to speak to your painful situation to bring healing and growth. But even with this, we may only ever make sense of our part. We will likely never fully understand why someone did what they did.

Since we live in a fallen world, there will always be unfair things that don't fit within our sense of justice. When we can't understand, we feel a loss of control. In our effort to find understanding and a sense of control, we create our own version of events to make sense of it. A counselor once shared with me that when we can't make sense of what happens, we conclude our experiences are the result of our own doing. While it is true that we often co-create our circumstances, sometimes we internalize and own behavior that has nothing to do with us. For example, victims of abuse may conclude they deserve abuse. This explanation makes sense of our experiences and gives us a sense of control, for if I can fix myself, then I can "control" whether the abuse happens or not. Or, if I can just compensate in other ways, perhaps I can convince that person to overlook my shortcomings and love me the way I long to be loved. In reality, there are painful things that happen to us that have little or nothing to do with us.

Chapter 6: How We Get Trapped in Our Thoughts

The event overrides the healing process.

Rumination steals our focus and prevents progress in our healing. We focus our energy on trying to "figure out" what happened instead of processing the emotions that resulted from what happened. The result is that healing becomes dependent upon figuring it out, resolving regret, or receiving some sort of restitution. Like my grieving co-worker, we become stuck in the event instead of moving forward through the healing process.

Accepting that we won't understand everything that happens to us is part of the healing process (and the essence of faith!). It's the part of the process where the Holy Spirit bridges the gap between what I can do to mend my soul and what only Jesus, the great soul Physician, can do. Ruminating on what happened and processing what happened are two entirely different things. Rumination is replaying and retelling. Processing is accepting, healing, and learning.

If you are prone to rumination, permit yourself to not think about a situation. Accept that you may never figure it out, you may never have all the answers you desire, and you will never be able to go back and change or control what happened. Those things don't invalidate what happened or how it affected you. If anything, they give credence to how you've felt about your experiences. You'll find your healing begins when you let go of your need to continually revisit what has happened or strive to make sense of it. Healing is a byproduct of trusting God with your pain.

② **Confirmation bias**

There was an element of truth to Elizabeth's third-grade experience. It WAS true that she didn't have the answer the teacher wanted. We can look at the situation objectively and see that many other things are also true—like that the teacher handled the situation poorly and that Elizabeth did the best she could when put on the spot. But we also know the enemy loves to take a morsel of truth and twist our perceptions so we arrive at inaccurate conclusions about our situation, ourselves, others, and even God.

Once we've formed a conclusion, such as "I'm not smart enough," we begin to gather evidence to support that conclusion subconsciously. This is called confirmation bias and describes the way we tend only to see what proves our existing beliefs and filter out experiences that might disprove them. Our ego likes to be proven right, so it feels satisfying to have experience validate what we believe—even if what we believe is a self-destructive lie. Remember, pride resists the work of truth in our lives.

As Elizabeth grew up, she gathered experiences that felt similar to third grade. With each occasion, the enemy said, "Aha, see, I was right about you. This experience proves it again!" Each time she went through the thought cycle, the stronghold became more reinforced. It grew bigger and claimed more territory in her life.

Just as a snowman is made by taking a ball of snow and packing layers of snow around it, the enemy uses "evidence" to build a stronghold. The original lie grows as our faulty interpretation of experiences reinforces the lie. The bigger the lie becomes, the more it builds momentum. More and more layers are added to the original, making the truth indistinguishable from the lie. And here's the really sneaky part: Because I recognize at least some of it is true, I conclude the entire snowball is truth.

THE SNOWBALL EFFECT

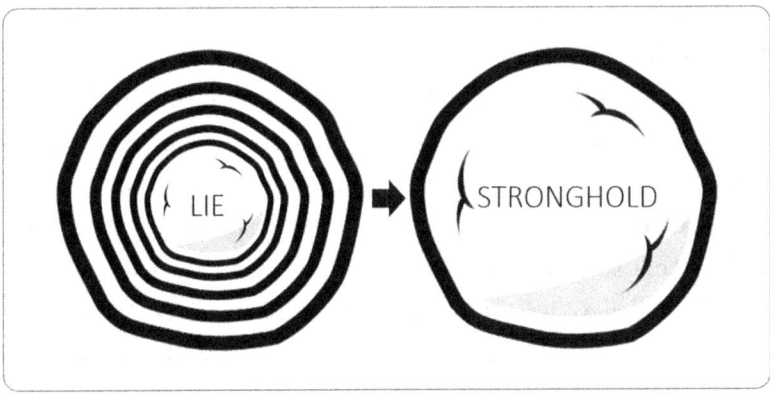

Just as snow sticks to snow, lies stick to lies. Deception opens the door to more deception. This also applies to truth. Mark 4:25 says, "*To those who listen to my teaching, more understanding will be given.*" Those who hear truth and apply it will receive greater levels of truth. Truth attracts more truth. Let's consider this on a practical level: If I eat lots of sugar, I crave sugar. If I eat lots of fruits and vegetables, I begin to crave healthy foods. What you feed yourself now will influence your cravings later. If I feed myself the truth, I will want more truth. If I accept lies, I'll fall prey to more of the same.

③ Unresolved anger

Anger serves a purpose in our lives. It is a natural emotion that arises when we feel threatened, attacked, or powerless, and is a response to our perception of injustice. It protects us from feeling what is below the anger, which is pain. Anger is easier to feel than other more vulnerable emotions, like rejection or betrayal. Temporary anger can be helpful and even help us get unstuck, as it may give us a boost of courage! Anger itself is not part of the problem. It is the anger we keep that keeps us stuck. The presence of unresolved anger is an indication of unhealed wounds from an event.

Paul urges us in Ephesians 4 to not let the sun go down on our anger because unresolved anger covers unresolved pain. It's not your anger that has you stuck, but rather what is beneath that anger. Over time, this pain evolves into resentment, which is the feeling that someone else owes us. And until that debt is "paid," we falsely believe we cannot move on with our lives. We become stuck in that place of indebtedness. Eventually, that unresolved resentment smolders and becomes a new stronghold—bitterness.

There is nothing that causes a standstill in a relationship more than anger, and this is certainly true of our relationship with the Lord. God knew, when He gave us free choice, that we would have anger towards Him at times. It comes with the territory of free choice. He was okay with that. It was worth the risk because it also meant we could have intimacy with Him. Just as we can't experience intimacy with God when we operate out of obligation (in the sense of religious duty), we cannot experience intimacy with God if He is obligated by our expectations to behave in a certain way. The moment we place terms or conditions on our relationship with the Lord, we are prone to being angry at Him. The demands we place on God create barriers to experiencing His love and power.

Think of unresolved anger as a callous. A callous creates a tough surface that protects the tender skin underneath. As a guitar player, I have well-developed callouses on the ends of the fingers on my left hand. These callouses have formed over years of playing guitar, where my fingertips press down on metal strings to create a clear tone. Many people set out to learn guitar but give up quickly because of the pain that is caused by making chords with your fingertips. It's an uncomfortable experience, but for those who press on (pun intended) and cross the threshold, it's very rewarding. *Note: Most rewarding experiences lie on the other side of a threshold!*

After years of playing guitar, I now have calloused fingertips that protect me from the feeling of pain. Those fingers can still feel some things, but the feeling is limited. Anger works in a similar fashion. Over time, it builds up into a callous on our hearts that protects us from feeling pain. We aren't entirely incapable of feeling, but our ability is limited. In other words, when we keep our anger, we go through life with a drastically limited ability to feel and experience life. Our angry and calloused hearts block out our ability to feel.

Some of us have befriended anger. We use it to keep others at arm's length, to create a buffer from painful situations, and as an excuse for our behavior. It ends up betraying us by perpetuating the very things we're trying to avoid. Others of us focus our energy on controlling or managing our anger. But if we're not free from anger, it is actually controlling us.

Here's the good news. From time to time, my callouses peel off, and I have to start again. Jesus wants to peel off the callouses on your heart. He's not mad at you for having anger; He simply desires to heal the pain that lies below your anger. He's not disgusted by your pain; He's drawn towards it. He was drawn toward the shame of the prostitute being judged. He went out of his way to show compassion to the woman at the well who was rejected. He returned to Judea to comfort Mary and Martha after the death of their brother Lazarus. Jesus has a habit of showing up where the pain is, and He'll show up for yours, too.

It's Time to Throw Off the Trap

You've likely heard someone say they are stuck in their own thoughts or that they "can't get out of their head." That's what strongholds do. God knew this would happen, so He provided a way out. 2 Corinthians 10:4 says, "*We use God's mighty weapons, not worldly weapons, to knock down the strongholds of human reasoning and to destroy false arguments.*" We may be human beings, but we don't use human plans, strategies, or methods to win our battles. There's a war for your thoughts and worldly weapons, like self-sufficiency, are sufficient. Spiritual battles must be fought with spiritual weapons. Our greatest spiritual weapon is truth.

Hebrews 12:1 commands us to throw aside the sin that entangles us. The word "entangles" refers to someone who desperately needs to advance but can't because they are encircled and trapped by something. The writer of Hebrews is comparing sin to a loosely fitting garment, like pants, that fall to the ground as the athlete runs. The pants become a hindrance to advancement. Thought traps keep you from advancing, but truth frees you from those traps.

Animals are known to do anything necessary to free themselves from traps—even to the point of chewing off their own leg. It's time for us to have that kind of commitment to our freedom (well, minus the chewing off your leg part). Getting unstuck means being honest about the thought patterns steering our lives, even if it's painful. It means accepting you've been deceived, even if it feels humiliating to do so. It means no longer dwelling on the offenses of the past, even if you haven't received the justice you desire. It means recognizing that our pride is preventing us from seeing situations as they are, even if the truth is scary. Finally, it means letting go of the anger that protects us from pain, even if that anger is our friend. It's time to get free.

PART THREE

How to Get Unstuck

CHAPTER 7

GETTING UNSTUCK IS A PROCESS

I can think of very few things in life that are not processes. Relationships, learning, career growth, skill development, and even faith is a process. It's the process that produces progress. We like to approach these things like they are formulas—if I do "this," then "that" will happen. This affinity for formulaic thinking creates an illusion of certainty, predictability, and control. It leads to frustration and disappointment when things don't happen like they think they *should*, and the formula fails us.

God does not work within a formula, but He does work within the process. Both formulas and processes have outcomes but are very different in other ways. A formula can be controlled, and we expect (even demand) God to cooperate. For example, if we pray a certain formulaic prayer, we expect to get a certain result. We like formulas because they are black-and-white, step-by-step, and give us a clear result. But since God doesn't work according to formulas, we are often disappointed when He does not deliver the result we expect, in the way we expect, or in the time frame we expect.

On the other hand, a process is a series of steps taken in order to get a certain result. Biblical prayer isn't a formula, but rather a process of trusting, surrendering, and engaging with the Father's heart about a situation. There is a theological basis for prayer achieving a particular end, but it's not as clear-cut or simple as a formula. It is much messier. We can't control a process; we can only cooperate.

There is no formula for getting unstuck. There is no way to avoid the mess or control the outcome. Getting stuck is a process and one that doesn't happen overnight. Before we look at the steps of the process, let's explore the value of engaging in God's processes.

His processes are always about what is to come.

God never initiates a process in your life without having something better in mind for you. Romans 8:31 says, *"If God is for us, who can ever be against us."* To be "for us" means He is for our benefit in every way and in everything He does; this includes His processes. A process may feel painful, but it is always for our benefit.

For every promise God gives, there is a process He will use to bring it about. This comes as no surprise—He's a God of Promise, and He's a God of Process. Every great man or woman of God has gone through His processes. David was anointed king, then had years of preparation before he took his throne. Joseph was promised he would rule over his brothers, then went through years of injustice where he was humbled and trained for leadership. Abraham received the promise of a son, then had to wait years for the promise to come true. God has you in a process because He is preparing you for a promise. Oh, and He's making you into a great man or woman of God, too!

We tend to resist His processes because they are difficult and costly. David was chased by his predecessor and betrayed by his best friend. Joseph was sold into slavery and ended up in prison after he was accused of things he didn't do. Abraham was asked to sacrifice the very promise he had waited for years to receive.

His processes are inconvenient, challenge our faith, and call us to new levels of humility. But His processes are ALWAYS for our good. According to Romans 8:28, He works all things for our good, which means He uses every aspect of the process to bring about His purposes. If you can trust the end result (that He's working all things for your good), then you can trust the process!

It is in that difficult process that He prepares you for what is to come. I don't give my car to my nine-year-old niece to drive. Why? Because she's not ready. There's a process of maturity and learning that needs to happen before she can steward that kind of gift and responsibility. It's for her benefit (and ours) that the process is required.

There's a promise waiting on the other side of your threshold, and the process of getting unstuck will prepare you to steward that promise. It will stretch you and transform you for greater things to come.

God works in the process more than He works in certain timing.

God doesn't think in terms of time as we do. Rather, He thinks in terms of process. He'll take all the time He needs to complete a process in me to bring about His desired result. Think about it: Growing a plant isn't about timing; it's about growing to maturity. A farmer harvests a crop when the plant has completed its process of growing grain. The byproduct of the process is a harvest. Time is only relevant to a plant because it expresses what is needed for a process to occur. Why is a farmer patient for a harvest? Because a farmer understands the principle of process.

God created time to serve us, create structure in our lives, and give us a way to measure our lives. At the same time, God isn't bound to time, and He exists outside of time. He's concerned about the fruit of the process more than the timing of it. We get impatient because we think in terms of timing instead of process. If I deliver on my promises on time at my job, I am considered reliable and trustworthy. By this definition, we believe God's trustworthiness is dependent upon timely delivery according to what we expect. No wonder we get so impatient. God's trustworthiness is best seen in His processes, not His timing.

There are many times when I've been in a hurry to get through a season or a process to get to the end result. In the Kingdom of God, the process is often more important than the end result. This is why I've often had to repeat those processes so God can do what He needs to do in me. When I resist the process, I delay the promise. If I take a shortcut, I get an incomplete result.

Recently, someone asked me about my plans for the future. I responded, "I'm not sure, I just know I'm not in a hurry to get there. I'm content to let God do in me what He needs to today." I'm learning to find Him in the process, regardless of His timing. We are not assured in Scripture that God will deliver according to our time frame, but we are assured that He will complete any process He initiates. Philippians 1:6 says, *"And I am certain that God, who began the good work within you, will continue his work until it is finally finished on the day when Christ Jesus returns."* God is faithful to lead you through the unstuck process to completion!

God leads the process, but we must yield to it.

You know when you have to acknowledge the terms and conditions before you can use a new software program? If we want to enjoy what Jesus has for us, we have to accept His terms and conditions. As soon as I begin to live under new terms and conditions, I'm ready for what comes next.

In Matthew 13, we read the parable of the sower, where Jesus uses four types of ground to illustrate what type of hearts produce harvests. Said another way, He uses types of farm ground to show us how we can cooperate with His growing process.

The first type of ground is the hard ground. In Biblical times, farmers with adjacent plots would share a common path to access their fields. Over time, these paths would become packed down due to daily foot traffic. This represents the hardness or pride of the heart. Pride resists truth, and hard hearts resist the planting of truth. There is no place for a seed to take root and produce a crop. These people refuse to engage in the process because they don't want to change.

The second type is the shallow ground. This soil appears to be fertile on the surface but isn't capable of sustaining life once the seed gets under the surface. We stunt our processes when we do not deal with the things that lie below the surface—like unforgiveness and bitterness. Instead of growing deep, sustaining roots, the truth dies because the shallow soil can't support the end result. These people like the idea of trusting the process but give up when things get difficult.

The third type is the thorny ground. This ground is unkept and allows weeds to overtake the intended crop. In other words, the process gets choked out by other influences, leaving no room for the seeds to grow. It's easy to give in to the expectations of others, the comfort of routine, and the familiarity of our current thoughts. These people quit the process because it's not worth the work to push through the opposition they face.

The final type is the fertile ground that grows a crop. This soil is a tender heart that is eager to participate in the process. The fertile soil yields to the work of the plow, which is the cultivating work of the Holy Spirit in our lives. It understands the plow's disruptive upheaval serves a purpose. The disruption is a crucial part of the process.

The hard, shallow, and thorny ground all resist the work of a plow and, therefore, don't produce the crop the sower intended to harvest. Only the fertile ground does. It's the same seed in each example; the difference is the soil's ability to support the process. We choose whether we resist the process or yield to it.

The process produces what is pleasing to God.

The messiest and ugliest processes produce the most beautiful results. Job 23:10 says, *"But he knows where I am going. And when he tests me, I will come out pure as gold."* When we trust His process, we come out pure as gold.

One season of my life where God was working overtime to get me unstuck, I was utterly overwhelmed by all of the sudden changes and losses in my life. I was starting to question why I had to go through so much—and so much at one time. I can remember seeing a vision in a time of prayer one evening. I saw hands wringing a wet towel until they had squeezed out the last drop of water. It stirred something in my heart—a desire to get every single drop of growth, blessing, and opportunity out of the process that I could. I knew I had to go through the process if I wanted what God had for me. There was no shortcut and no way around it. So, if I had to go *through* it, I wanted everything God had for me *in* it. Instead of asking God to end the process,

I prayed that God would teach me how to make the most of the process.

We may not know what lies on the other side of our threshold, but we are assured that His process of getting us unstuck will produce some predictable and worthwhile results, such as:

- **Intimacy with Him** – We tend to look for proof of God's love in the end result, but it's in the process that we find intimacy. I've discovered we can lose many things in the process of getting unstuck—friendships, jobs, ministries, even reputations can be lost. But what we gain in intimacy with the Father cannot be lost or taken from us. He's our treasure, and a treasure we get to keep!
- **Christlikeness** – You will emerge looking more like Christ. Just as the pressure of a potter's hand shapes a piece of clay, it is the pressure of the process that forms Christ in us.
- **Wisdom** – You'll be wiser the next time around and learn to identify the lies and pitfalls that get you stuck more quickly. The wisdom you gain through this process will benefit you the rest of your life—and God will use what you learn through your process to help others through their own!

When you are feeling discouraged or overwhelmed in the process, remember this: You can trust the process because you can trust God. Just like wringing a wet towel produces a predictable result, you can be assured that God will maximize your process for your benefit and His glory.

Introduction to the Unstuck Process

I can't tell you exactly how to get unstuck in your particular situation, but I've found in my own life that the process of getting unstuck involves these four steps:

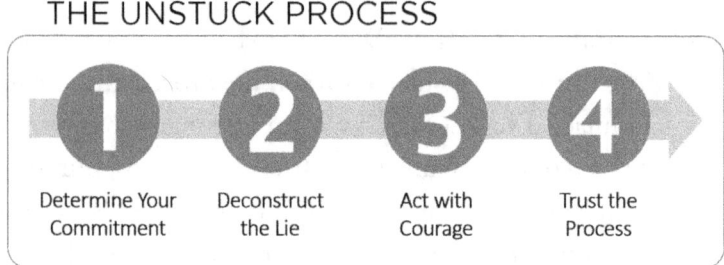

We'll dive into each step in the coming pages, but first, I want to remind you of some key points:

- Success in the Kingdom of God is forward progress and growth.
- This isn't a formula—it's a process. You can't control it, only cooperate with it.
- Your process will look a little different for you than it did for me. That's okay.
- There's no set timing for any stage, but they work best when done in order.
- Each step will require greater levels of surrender and trust in the Lord.

CHAPTER 8

DETERMINE YOUR COMMITMENT

We identify a person's commitment by their behaviors. But, like everything else we've discussed so far, commitment begins with our thought-life. The first step in the process is to examine your current commitments and clearly determine your future ones.

You've stayed at this mountain long enough.
The Old Testament story of the Israelites resonates deeply with me, perhaps because I can see so much of my journey mirrored in theirs. They are people who had clear promises from God and regularly witnessed incredible miracles—yet they still struggled to trust and obey. Over and over again, they got into messes that only God could get them out of. God gave us their story as a clear picture of how He leads us through the process of getting unstuck.

We'll pick up with the Israelites just after being delivered from 400 years of slavery in Egypt. They had seen God part the Red Sea on their behalf to seal their new freedom and had made it to the area of Mount Sinai, where they had lived for the past year. You could argue this was the peak of God's people thus far in history, so it seems like an unlikely place they would get stuck. We often get stuck after a failure, but sometimes we get stuck after a victory. We've all known someone who is reliving their high school glory days or is still clinging to what worked 10 years ago, right? My point is that both failures and successes can open the door for deception. We can get stuck on the mountaintop, in the valley, and anywhere in between. This is why we must guard our thought-life with vigilance at all times.

It was in the shadow of Mount Sinai that God prompted the Israelites to move on in their journey to the promised land of Canaan. He speaks through Moses in Deuteronomy 1:6–7, *"When we were at Mount Sinai, the Lord our God said to us, 'You have stayed at this mountain long enough. It is time to break camp and move on…'"* In this speech, Moses is preparing the people to enter the Promised Land by recounting what God said at the beginning of their journey. Sometimes we need to be reminded of what He has promised so we will move forward with confidence.

Not everyone wanted to go, as the area around Mount Sinai had become home. It was here they were transformed from a group of misfits who had escaped Egypt into a unified nation with a purpose and a promise. They were given the Ten Commandments to govern their new lives and learned how to steward the Presence of God by building the tabernacle. And it was here that God once again asked them to pack up and move on. They had stayed in this place long enough. In Hebrew, this means "long enough for you." In other words, the season had served its purpose for the Israelites. The process had prepared them, and now it was time to move on.

No matter how good that mountain had been to them, if they stayed put, they would never reach the Promised Land. They were at a crossroads, a point of decision, a threshold. The same is true for you and me. There will be times in our lives where we must, by faith, walk away from something good in order to obtain the promise that remains ahead for us. Some things in our lives are meant to be seasons, but when we set up camp and build our lives around them, we get stuck in that season. Instead, God intends for us to move from season to season, which is one of the ways we grow and progress. It's tempting to let what is temporary become permanent. You might even be stuck because you've turned a season into a permanent residence. Good things can become thresholds, too.

There are people, situations, churches, jobs, and opportunities that are meant for your training but are not intended to be long-term. Similarly, sometimes people set up camp in your life, only to break camp and move on. This isn't a failure on your part or theirs. They served their purpose, and you accomplished yours. Even when relationships are severed in painful or ungodly ways, God will take what you learned and use it for good in your next season.

So often, we hold on to the place or thing designed to prepare us for what comes next. Ironically, it keeps us from embracing the very thing we are being prepared for. This is hard for our hearts to understand, as we mourn leaving a season we've loved. What God is doing in your life today is always preparation for what He will do in your life tomorrow. This mountain was the place where the Israelites received the Law, which became the framework for how they would relate to God and to one another. What they obtained at the mountain was crucial to their ability to steward what came next—the Promised Land. When we view a season as a time of preparation and learning, we can honor what God has done in the past while still looking forward.

There's another way we turn something temporary into something permanent—and this may be more dangerous than the first. This occurs when we justify a behavior, believing it is a short-term way to cope with a situation. Instead, it becomes a permanent stronghold in our lives. For example, there have been stressful seasons in my life where I have justified unhealthy eating by telling myself it would only be for a short season—you know, just to get through this difficult time. But those mindsets only repeated themselves the next time things got hard. What I convinced myself would only be temporary became a lasting cycle. What I convinced myself would be beneficial for a season became destructive when it became a cycle. We all learn "ways of dealing with life" that help us at the moment but become thresholds down the road.

If you are stuck, then you have stayed at this place long enough. If you want to get unstuck, you'll have to break camp. What season, relationship, or habit do you need to leave behind to embrace what comes next? What are you doing to cope with life that is instead keeping you from thriving in life?

Fill in the blank: I have been _____ too long.

It's time to break camp and move on.

Moses didn't mince words when he commanded the people to break camp and move on. To "break camp" means to pull up the stakes of your tents and pack up so you can advance to a new place. The Hebrew word for "move on" means to turn and do something different. It is a verb of motion, movement, or action. In other words, getting unstuck requires some sort of new action or behavior, and often one that is unfamiliar, uncomfortable, and has an unknown outcome. It is one thing to recognize and acknowledge you've been stuck on your mountain long enough. It's another thing to act upon it. This is the place where most people get stuck in being stuck. They don't like being stuck, but the change required is too daunting or costs too much.

There are some important questions to ask yourself to break camp and move on. You must answer these questions as honestly as you can, without any sugarcoating or justification. Your ability to be authentic is essential to your journey. Your answers will give you a starting place for your journey. The answers to these questions will also help you determine your readiness to move on. Not everyone wants to get unstuck.

Here are three powerful questions to ask yourself:

QUESTION #1: What is my threshold?

What is it that is truly holding you back? As the Holy Spirit begins to reveal thresholds to you, these revelations may sting a little. I'm not trying to scare you off. On the contrary, I want to encourage you to embrace the sting because it is going to lead you somewhere. When the Holy Spirit is involved, discomfort always leads you somewhere.

My niece loves animals. Furry, slimy, feathery, even scaly... she likes them all. She also believes if she names something, it becomes hers—regardless of whether it is supposed to be a household pet or not. Once, when I was in her bedroom, I noticed she had several sticky notes lined up on her wall with words written on them. I asked her what they were for, and she replied that they were names of future pets. After all, you never know when you're going to find a frog that needs a name! The girl is a real planner!

There is significance to naming something. It takes courage to label the things you've denied, ignored, or justified. It takes courage to admit you believe a lie and that the lie is keeping you stuck. It's gutsy to take an honest assessment of your current camp and give it a name. But when you can call it what it is, you can deal with what it is.

Naming your threshold brings it into the light.

Ephesians 5:13–14 says intentions are exposed in the light. If you wake up in the middle of the night to take the dog out, you don't stumble through the darkness. You turn the light on so you can find your way. Otherwise, you end up stubbing your toe! Similarly, if you want to find your way out of being stuck, you need to shine the light on the situation. If your intention has been to protect yourself with your behaviors, you can shine the light on it by calling it what it is—no excuses, no fluff, and no spin. If your intention has been to keep anger so you don't have to deal with the pain that lies beneath the anger, call it what it is. If your intention has been to choose an addictive behavior so you can avoid dealing with things that happened in your childhood, call it what it is.

As long as it stays in the dark, it can grow, fester, and control your life. If you get sick because of something that is in your house, it is likely something that is either hidden or living in the dark, such as mold or mildew. Nothing good ever grows in the dark. It can be scary to bring things into the light, but it's also freeing. The moment you give it a name is the moment you can start doing something about it. Maybe it's time we start writing the lies we believe on sticky notes. Then we will have to address them!

Chapter 8: Determine Your Commitment

In Mark 5:1–5, Jesus encounters a man who is filled with demons and crying out for help. It was the tormented cry of a person who was hurting and stuck in a hopeless situation. No one had been able to help him in his condition—not friends, family, doctors, or even religious leaders. Because of his condition, he lived in the city graveyard and made his home in one of the tombs. He was naked, wailed constantly, cut himself with sharp stones, and could not be controlled. This is a man who was stuck in his condition.

While I believe in the existence and power of demons, we may relate to this man in other even more relevant ways. Perhaps you are stuck in addiction and have lost control of your life. Perhaps you have made your home in a graveyard, stuck in a place of loss and broken-heartedness. Or perhaps you are stuck in a cyclical behavior that no doctor, pastor, or expert has been able to free you from. But Jesus can. Something deep inside this man's spirit knew Jesus was the way to get unstuck because when he sees Him from a long way off, he runs to Him.

I love that Jesus stops teaching, turns from the crowd, and focuses on this man who was the shame of the city and who had long ago been given up on. He does the same for us. That's how much Jesus desires to meet us in our "stuck" condition to bring us freedom! Immediately, Jesus discerns the presence of demons who are keeping this man bound and says to the spirits in verse nine, *"'What is your name?' He said, 'My name is Many, for there are many of us.'"* Why do you suppose Jesus asks the demon his name? Surely Jesus already knew. And surely Jesus could have cast it out even without knowing his name. Jesus asked his name to expose him for what he truly was.

There's a popular and true saying that says when you bring something into the light, it takes away its power. This is a profound Biblical truth. The darkness hates the light because of the light's power to expose. John 3:20 says, *"All who do evil hate the light and refuse to go near it for fear their sins will be exposed."* The enemy hates truth because it exposes his lies. He will work overtime to keep you in darkness and to keep your lie nameless. Exposing a lie is the beginning of taking back your power over that threshold.

The man is set free, restored to wholeness, and returned to his right mind. But he soon discovers that getting unstuck was only the beginning of his journey. It's what comes after getting unstuck that often catches the attention of others. Mark goes on to tell us the man went away and told everyone in the land what Jesus had done for him. Things that are brought into the light grow into something great that others can see. This man not only got healed, but he shared his story of being healed with everyone he encountered. It makes me wonder how many other people sought Jesus out to see if He could help them in response to his story. When you experience freedom and breakthrough from a threshold, it becomes your testimony. It becomes your story of God's goodness. When you get unstuck, it will be contagious to the people around you.

Naming your threshold makes it yours to own.

We know, deep down, that if we admit our threshold, we must do something about it. As long as we remain distanced from it, we can choose to ignore it. But once you've named it, you can now own it. It's kind of like when you have a baby at the hospital and the nurses ask you for a name to list on the birth certificate. As a parent, you have the legal right to assign a name to your baby. Ownership and naming go hand in hand (just ask my niece). And you know what else? After you name that baby,

Chapter 8: Determine Your Commitment

they make you take it home and care for it! This ownership is what makes parenting both terrifying and exciting. The same is true for owning your threshold. It is terrifying because it means you must now act upon it in some way, but it's also exciting because it means you are stepping into a new adventure. And just like parenting, you don't need to know everything to get started. You'll learn along the way.

Jesus pressed the crippled man at the Pool of Bethesda (John 5:15) with the question, *"Do you want to be well?"* before He granted his healing. In this single question, Jesus exposes a victim mentality (a lie). The man responds he couldn't possibly receive healing because no one would help him down to the pool. After years of seeing others get healed and being passed by, his lie had snowballed into a stronghold. I don't blame him; it *seemed* like the truth.

As soon as the man provided his excuse, his threshold was named and it was his to own. In exposing this mindset, Jesus empowers the man to cross his threshold of unbelief and lay hold of his healing. He was committed to getting well, but he was also committed to his victim mentality. Now he had to choose which one he would be most committed to—and in doing so, cross a threshold. He must have realized this, as he doesn't hesitate to obey Jesus in the next moment by picking up his mat and walking. No one can pick up your mat and walk for you. Notice that Jesus doesn't do it for him. Jesus won't cross your threshold for you, but He will give you everything you need to take the step.

It's time to name your threshold and take care of it. Why do I really do what I do? What am I really afraid of? What do I really want? Do I really want to be well? What am I most committed to? It requires being ruthlessly honest with yourself about what is holding you back. We all have a threshold; the question is, does it own you, or will you own it?

Naming your threshold gives you a plan.

A couple of years ago, I had a cough and congestion that just wouldn't go away. I enjoy going to the doctor about as much as I enjoy running (okay, I hate both), so I put off a trip to the doctor as long as I possibly could, hoping the sickness would go away on its own. I even looked up my symptoms on the internet and discovered I might have a common cold or could possibly be dying, or anything in between. After several weeks of hoping it would disappear, I finally gave in. A five-minute wait in the waiting room (a miracle in itself) and a ten-minute visit with a doctor soon gave me a diagnosis that I had a severe sinus infection and needed antibiotics. Within a couple of days, my congestion had subsided. Here's my point: The moment my illness had a name, it then had a treatment. As long as it remained unnamed, all I could do was try over-the-counter medicine and buy tissues in bulk to keep up. But the moment it had a name, I had a plan for dealing with it.

When you put a name to your thought trap, you begin to catch your thoughts. When you put a name to an addiction, you can create a recovery plan. When you put a name to an unhealthy relationship, you can begin to implement boundaries. When you put a name on a lie, you can exchange it for truth. A name precedes a plan.

Once you've named your threshold, you can work with the Holy Spirit to create a plan of action for moving through your threshold. It's incredibly empowering to get to this point, especially if you have been stuck for a long time. For every possible way you can get stuck, He has a way for you to get out.

My prayer is that He'll use this book as part of His plan to help you get free!

As part of that process, you begin to explore what possibilities can come from facing your threshold. There are several synonyms for "brought to light" that include reveal, expose, uncover, disclose, and unearth. But there's one synonym that really caught my attention: discover. Once something is brought to light, you can discover the truth about it. You can discover what God has to say about it. You can discover what is on the other side of your threshold. You can discover what comes next.

**REFLECTION QUESTION: My threshold is _____
_____.**

QUESTION #2: What am I gaining by staying stuck?
The second question to ask yourself is, "What am I gaining by staying stuck in this place?" A threshold serves a purpose, or else it wouldn't have a place in our lives. We established in previous chapters that at the root of your area of "stuck" is a lie you believe about yourself, your situation, others, or God. You are gaining something by believing that lie, or else you wouldn't believe it.

Lies always serve a purpose. If I believe I am unlovable, it protects me from having to step into intimacy with the Lord and with others. If I believe I am a failure, it protects me from having to take risks or taking responsibility. If I believe I am not responsible, it protects me from seeing my role in a situation. Lies are convenient, or we wouldn't keep them around. We fall for the illusion that believing a lie is beneficial for us!

Just as the serpent's lie served Eve's ego, Satan crafts lies that will serve a need in you. He studies you, your patterns, and your insecurities and crafts customized lies, which he delivers in your moments of weakness. This is why it is so crucial that we give Jesus full access to our lives and fill ourselves with His Word. It fills in the cracks that the enemy wants to occupy. Water in a crack in concrete will freeze and expand, causing the crack to grow and damage the cement. When we have unmet needs in our souls, the enemy fills them with lies to temporarily meet those needs. They gradually and subtly expand and grow, causing damage to our lives in the process. What meets our needs at the moment causes great damage over time. What you gain by remaining stuck is costing you more than you realize. That lie is robbing you blind.

Our attachments meet a need.

How quickly we become attached to our beliefs, behaviors, routines, relationships, familiarities, and even our dysfunctions! But here's the truth about attachments: You can't attach to the new while hanging on to the old. For example, if your hands are full, you can't pick up anything new until you first set something down. The same holds true for us. We can't pick up the new thing God has for us if we won't first let go of the old. One of the greatest impediments to growth is an unhealthy attachment.

The lie of attachment says we can't let go of something because it meets a need, and we can't afford to have that need not be met. The deeper lie of attachment is a fear that the need won't be met if we let go and trust God with it. This kind of attachment is a form of self-sufficiency.

Jesus's encounter with a rich young ruler is a Scriptural example of how our attachments meet our soulish needs but keep us from trusting God. "*As Jesus was starting out on his way to Jerusalem, a man came running up to him, knelt down, and asked, 'Good Teacher, what must I do to inherit eternal life?' 'Why do you call me good?' Jesus asked. 'Only God is truly good'*" (Mark 10:17–18).

Why does Jesus ask this disarming question—especially when this man was correct in calling Him a good teacher? He kneels and refers to Him as a good teacher, which is more than the Pharisees of the day did. You wouldn't think Jesus would reprimand him for this! But it is because Jesus knew that while this man respected and admired Him, he was not ready to surrender. He recognized Jesus as good, but not as Lord. Many people respect the teachings of Jesus and admire His works, but they aren't ready to let Him be the Lord of their lives. It costs us nothing to admire Jesus. It costs us everything to follow Him.

The word "inherit" means to acquire by sonship. This rich young ruler knew a great deal about inheritance and acquiring things. The account in Luke calls him a ruler, which implied that he was a well-respected ruler among the Jewish people. It is likely he inherited his wealth, so he had never known anything but a life of comfort, which allowed him to acquire anything he wanted in life—except the assurance of eternal life.

Jesus responds to his question about eternal life by quoting the Ten Commandments he must follow. *"'Teacher,' the man replied, 'I've obeyed all these commandments since I was young'"* (Mark 10:20). This young man viewed this list from the commandments as a checklist of actions—another way to acquire what he wanted. Jesus viewed the list as an examination of the condition of his heart. You can "keep" the commandments as a checklist (I didn't murder anyone today…check!) without having a relationship with Jesus. But you can't keep the commandments in the way Jesus described without His Lordship over your life (I may not have murdered anyone today, but I did get angry with someone, which Matthew 5:22 describes as the equivalent of murder in my heart).

"Looking at the man, Jesus felt genuine love for him. 'There is still one thing you haven't done,' he told him. 'Go and sell all your

possessions and give the money to the poor, and you will have treasure in heaven. Then come, follow me'" (Mark 10:21). I love the glimpse we get of Jesus's character here. Standing in front of Him is a man who doesn't get it and yet Jesus only felt love for him. He wasn't disgusted, frustrated, or impatient. He didn't send him away. No, instead, He stayed with it and invited this man into a relationship with Him. I'm glad for this, as I often don't "get it" either.

It's at this point that Jesus asks him for his attachments in exchange for a relationship with Him, just like He asks us. It's important to note that this man's riches represented far more than financial security. Wealth represented status, importance, and power—and the only identity he had known, which had served him well. It got him many things in life, likely even earning him friendships and admirers. And now Jesus asks for it. *"At this, the man's face fell, and he went away sad, for he had many possessions"* (Mark 10:22).

Jesus asked him for his attachment. He asked him to give up his entire identity in order to take on a new one as a son of God. Jesus's answer flipped the script on how the thought-life should work. But because the rich young ruler didn't want to give up his attachments, he sulked and walked away. His fear of losing his inheritance kept him from gaining a new eternal inheritance.

The story of the rich young ruler is included in three of the four Gospels, which tells me God wants us to have a deep understanding of where our attachments lie (pun intended). Jesus wasn't after his money. Jesus was after his heart. Mark continues, *"Jesus looked around and said to his disciples, '…it is very hard to enter the Kingdom of God. In fact, it is easier for a camel to go through the eye of a needle than for a rich person to enter the Kingdom of God!'"* (Mark 10:23). When Jesus says it is hard for the rich to enter the Kingdom of God, He's not talking about wealth. He's talking about people who have attachments that have such a high value assigned to them they are unwilling to bring them under the Lordship of Jesus. He was asking the man, "What are you most committed to—me, or your money and importance?" Your threshold is always an issue of Lordship. It may be financial wealth and material goods. But it might also be our "right" to be angry at someone or our desire to be accepted by others. I am confident of this: You cannot get unstuck without letting go of something.

Grief is part of the surrender process.

Because surrender is initially the loss of something you've held on to, you will grieve as part of your process. It is natural to grieve, and even miss, the very thing we are surrendering. This is not a breach of the surrender process. It is, instead, an opportunity to once again invite the Holy Spirit into our process. The Holy Spirit is our comforter. Some of us never experience that side of Him because we never open ourselves up to the need to be comforted by embracing loss and grief. The tragedy is that we have more confidence in the ability of food, busyness, medication, and friends to comfort us than we do the very Godhead that embodies comfort. He doesn't just comfort. He IS comfort. Here are some examples of grief you may experience as you get unstuck:

- If you are surrendering unforgiveness, you will grieve what may have been lost or stolen from you in a relationship. We often must grieve what was or what could have been in order to prepare our hearts for what can and will be.
- If you are surrendering a promise God has given you, you will grieve your expectations about when and how He will make the promise come to pass. Think of Abraham

taking his promised son up to the mountain to sacrifice him. I can only imagine he was overcome with grief as he surrendered his long-awaited promise back to God!
- If you are surrendering insecurity, you will grieve what that insecurity has provided you. Perhaps that insecurity has protected you or allowed you to isolate yourself. Or perhaps that insecurity has allowed you to live a safe and predictable life.

Have you ever noticed how God will shift your affections towards something or someone so you are prepared to let go when it's time? I've had friends say their children became most annoying right before leaving for college, which made it much easier to let them go! Have you noticed how He will surface old things right before a new season to give you the opportunity to find closure? Perhaps you'll cross paths with a person who had wronged you, giving you an opportunity for closure. These are examples of how the Holy Spirit leads us into grieving so we can transition to the next season.

God's exchange policy

Somewhere along the way, we've created a department store return policy view of God. If I buy a pair of pants but get them home and decide I don't like them, I can return them to the store. One option is to exchange them for an item of equal or lesser value. We believe God operates the same way: If I give up an attachment, maybe God will give me something in return that is of equal or lesser value. No! That's not the way God works at all! If God were a department store, He would work like this: I would take my ratty, torn-up, stained jeans that aren't worth anything to me to the returns counter. God would greet me with a huge grin

Chapter 8: Determine Your Commitment

and tell me He is so very pleased I'm ready to make an exchange. As I hand Him my old jeans, He would graciously take them and offer in exchange the nicest pair of jeans in the store. You see, God doesn't exchange our attachments for things that are of equal or lesser value. When we give something of earthly value to God, He ALWAYS gives us something back of greater Kingdom value! Every. Single. Time.

Luke 14:33 says you cannot become His disciple without giving up everything you own. Discipleship is an exchange that costs you everything. In fact, if your walk with the Lord doesn't cost you anything, then it isn't discipleship at all. The greatest exchange is that we die to ourselves, and we get His life in exchange. The cross is the guarantee for His exchange policy.

My tendency is to straddle the line—I want to keep my pride, my preferences, and my protections AND have what God wants for me. But it doesn't work that way. I imagine my spiritual walk has often looked like a terrible game of Twister! I do my best to contort my life so I don't have to surrender anything, all while trying to lay hold of what God has. Inevitably, a game of Twister results in the players being stuck in position, unable to move or reach new spots without collapsing.

Every time you come to a place of surrender, God develops something in you that can't be stolen. It changes the way you think, feel, and behave from the inside out. He apprehends our hearts through surrender, and we, in turn, apprehend His. I can think of no greater exchange than that.

REFLECTION QUESTIONS

What am I gaining by staying stuck?
_____
_____
_____
_____
_____

What might I "lose" (earthly value) when I get unstuck?
_____
_____
_____
_____
_____

What might I "gain" (Kingdom value) by getting unstuck?
_____
_____
_____
_____
_____

QUESTION #3: What am I MOST committed to?

Let's return to the journey of the Israelites, who pack up camp and leave for Canaan. They come to Kadesh Barnea, where Moses commissions the twelve spies to go into Canaan, the land given to them, to scout it out. The spies go in and see that the land is exactly as God described it—full of milk and honey, symbols of provision and abundance. The land is everything God promised them it would be! But they also see the land is filled with giants. It's a threshold of epic (or giant) proportions. This wasn't part of the deal. No one told them there would be giants. No one told them there would be a process to attaining the promise!

Two of the spies believe they should take the land, but ten are afraid and warn the people of the danger. In response, the entire group falls into fear, and they remain stuck outside of the Promised Land for the next 40 years until every adult who refused to trust God dies. Their rejection of the process caused them to miss out on the promise.

We learn from this example of how the enemy exaggerates what you see to create fear. Believing these fear-causing lies keeps you from God's best, just as we saw fear keep Adam from fellowship with God. The Israelites threshold was not the giants, for God had promised to give them the victory and the land. Their threshold was their thinking about the giants. Check out what the spies reported back to the Israelites after coming back from Canaan in Number 13:33, *"Next to them, we felt like grasshoppers, and that's what they thought, too!"* You'll never occupy your promises with a grasshopper mindset! The Israelites wanted the Promised Land, but they wanted safety more. They wanted the milk and honey but feared the giants more. They were committed to the Promised Land, but they were MOST committed to avoiding the unknowns of Canaan!

I've heard it said our lives are perfectly designed to get the results we get. Sometimes we're stuck because we are more committed to being stuck than we are to the work of getting unstuck. We're more loyal to the lie, or rather the comfort and familiarity of the lie than we are to pursuing what God has for us. Maybe we don't want to upset others. Maybe we're afraid of what will happen if we change our behavior. Maybe we are more committed to our current behavior than we are to getting unstuck.

John's Story: Stuck in Rejection

John grew up in a home with a domineering father and a distant mother. No matter what he did, he couldn't live up to his father's impossible standards or earn his mother's affection. Because of this, a stronghold of rejection formed in his thinking. He believed the lie he was worthless and began acting weird at school so the other kids would stay at a distance. Though he loved sports, he didn't try out for the baseball team because he couldn't bear the thought of being rejected again.

The unhealed pain of his childhood continued into adulthood. His fear of rejection kept everyone in his life at arm's length. Though he wanted badly to be married, he would find a petty reason to break off the relationship every time things started to get serious. He rejected others before they rejected him.

In his mid-30s, he experienced love and acceptance for the first time when a co-worker introduced him to Jesus. As he began to experience God's love, he was finally able to face the pain of his childhood. His stronghold of rejection had served a purpose in his life; it seemed to protect him from the pain of being rejected again but it actually kept him from experiencing love and acceptance. John realized he had been more committed to his rejection than he was to finding a lasting, healthy relationship and invited Jesus to give him the healing he needed to cross his threshold.

Because he had rejected others for most of his life, it took a while for John to learn how to have

> real relationships. He was unlearning old behaviors and learning new ones, like conflict management, vulnerability, and trust. These new behaviors were scary, but John was now more committed to relationship than he was to protecting himself from rejection. After a season of deep healing and growing, John was free from fear of rejection and ready to love and be loved.

Our threshold is a decision about the place of our commitment. We may not find out what we are most committed to until our back is to the wall and we are faced with a hard decision. It is in these moments that I'm learning to make decisions that align with who I want to be and what I want long-term, rather than what feels most familiar or safe at the moment. John made the decision to abandon what felt safe for the long-term goal of relationships. Let's look at how John's decision affected his trajectory.

JOHN'S DECISION POINT

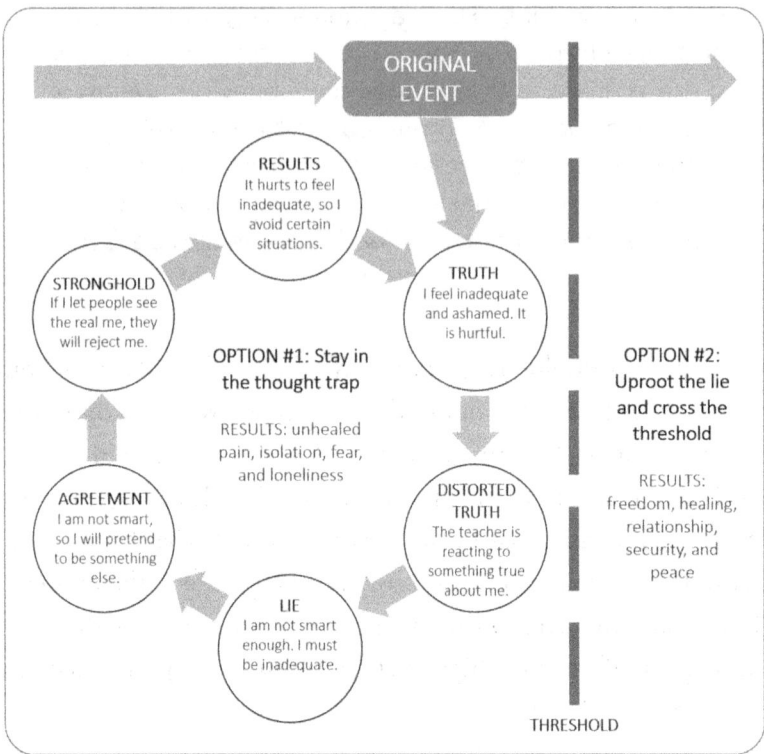

Crossing a threshold is choosing what you want most over what you want at the moment. We all have areas in our lives where we choose something that has a short-term payoff at the expense of a long-term benefit. When you answer the question, "What am I most committed to?" the brutal honesty of that answer should step on your toes a little. If it doesn't hurt, you're probably still lying to yourself. Here are some common examples of misplaced commitments that get us stuck:

- I am committed to developing a deeper relationship with the Lord, BUT I am more committed to my busyness.

- I am committed to stewarding money, BUT I am more committed to having what I want when I want it.
- I am committed to loving people, BUT I am more committed to being right.
- I am committed to my family, BUT I am more committed to the importance I get from my career.
- I am committed to being healthy, BUT I am more committed to glazed donuts.
- I am committed to authentic relationships, BUT I am more committed to protecting myself from hurt.
- I am committed to healthy relationships, BUT I am more committed to keeping the peace.
- I am committed to stepping out and using my talents, BUT I am more committed to comfort.
- I am committed to changing my circumstances, BUT I am more committed to my victim mentality.

Perhaps you can relate to one or more of those statements. Whatever you are most committed to is the lord of your life. We *want* to be committed to making Jesus the Lord of our life, but our own misplaced commitments keep us from experiencing the superb reality of His Lordship. *Spoiler alert:* His Lordship will always lead you out of stuck places.

The tragedy in the story of the Israelites is that a misplaced commitment kept an entire generation from entering the Promised Land. Though the tribe would eventually enter Canaan, all but two of the original group died before experiencing what God had for them. A misplaced commitment is a lie that has become a threshold.

REFLECTION QUESTION: I am committed to getting unstuck, BUT I've been more committed to _____
_____.

After deciding not to take the land, the Israelites began to murmur and conspire to find a new leader who would take them back to Egypt (Numbers 14:4). They wanted to be free from Egypt, but they wanted the safety of the former status quo even more. The reason it is so crucial you answer the question about what you are most committed to is because your commitment will be tested during your process of getting unstuck. You will be tempted to return to what feels familiar.

If we were all a little more honest about our commitments—both with ourselves and with others—it would create the kind of clarity, transparency, and accountability we need to get and stay unstuck! Since our true commitments can often be cloaked in excuses or justification, here are a couple of ideas for how to identify what your true commitments are:

Do an honest assessment of your patterns

I had a college professor who would often say you can know people by their patterns. Your patterns, including habits, tell the story of your life. Over time, your patterns begin to paint a clear picture of who you are, and most importantly, what you believe and value. They reveal your true commitments.

Your patterns will tell a story about your habits and your cyclical behavior. For example, a pattern of self-destruction tells a story about shame. Recurring jealousy tells a story about insecurity. A pattern of bitterness tells a story about unhealed wounds. A habit of worry tells a story about fear. It also works in reverse. A pattern of joy tells a story about trust in God. Integrity tells the story of a person's character. A track record of follow-through tells a story of dependability. Your patterns describe your life.

Every pattern of behavior is steered under the surface by a pattern of thoughts. When you do an honest assessment of your patterns, it will give you an honest evaluation of your thought-life. Quality thoughts (truth) produce quality patterns. Unhealthy thoughts (lies) produce unhealthy patterns.

> **Kristy's Story: Stuck in Striving**
>
> Kristy experienced great business success at a young age. She was ambitious and driven, and savvy in the business world. These qualities appeared like an admirable quality on the surface, but those working closely with her often felt uneasy. They didn't fully trust her motives. This resulted in a pattern of business success but with strained relationships. It was confusing to her how she could have such a track record of success and genuinely want the same for others but still struggle to build trust with her co-workers. They liked her but didn't trust her—and no one could quite put their finger on why. Her frustration with this pattern led her to ask the Holy Spirit to show her what was going on under the surface.
>
> Kristy had a rough childhood. She was born to drug addicts, was in and out of foster care, and ended up being adopted by a hyper-religious family. She spent her teenage years rebelling and being alienated from her adoptive family. Though she had been radically saved soon after high school and had received much emotional healing since then, there was shame and pain that lingered under the surface. Understandably

> so. What she didn't realize is how much that shame and pain fueled her ambition. They steered her towards opportunities that would allow her to prove herself and prove that she wasn't just the child of addicts. They drove her to work long hours at the expense of her relationship with her husband and daughter.
>
> The Holy Spirit revealed she believed a lie that she had to achieve success to prove herself, to prove she wasn't like her birth parents. This hidden motive was what her co-workers sensed when they were uneasy around her, and it fueled her patterns at work and home. Once Kristy realized she needed healing in the place of that lie, she repented and invited the Holy Spirit to come and do His work. Almost immediately, her relationships with co-workers improved. Not only that, but God gave her the opportunity to re-establish a relationship with her birth father, bringing her even deeper healing! She's still ambitious and successful, but now it comes from a place that builds healthy relationships and produces better results.

So, what story do your patterns tell? If you don't like your answer to that question, here's the good news: You can always learn new patterns! Jesus came to the earth to become a new pattern for us to model our lives after. In doing so, He empowered us to live like Him. Everything Jesus is, He empowers us to become.

REFLECTION QUESTION: What are the three predominant patterns in my life, and what do they reveal about my thinking?

1. _____

_____

_____

Chapter 8: Determine Your Commitment

2. _____

3. _____

Pay attention to your reactions

Have you ever walked away from a bothersome situation and thought, "Why did I react that way?" or "Why did I say that?" Our reactions reveal our commitments and serve as great indicators of what is going on below the surface. The Israelites reacted to the giants in Canaan with fear, revealing a gap in their faith. Their faith was strong enough to lead them out of a scary situation in Egypt but not strong enough to lead them into a scary one, even though victory was assured. Canaan revealed faulty thinking in them that Egypt did not. It's amazing how motivated we are to trust Him when we're in a pickle. It's a different story to trust Him to lead us into one!

I have found many times over the years that the Holy Spirit uses my reactions to situations to get my attention. He gives me a Canaan experience to reveal a gap so I'm willing to deal with something I've been avoiding. Recently, I felt convicted about some things I said in a conversation with a friend. I realized I had reacted from a place of insecurity and said some prideful things to cover that insecurity. At first, I felt ashamed of my behavior because it's not a reflection of who I want to be. I had demonstrated that I was more committed to my ego than I was to loving my friend. The Holy Spirit was using it as a gift so I could see what was truly in my heart: a lie I believed. Once He exposed this area of deception, I was able to experience His truth in that place.

I've also noticed this: Reactions generally come from the deception we believe, but responses come from a place of truth. If I believe the lie that God won't defend me, I must react defensively. If I believe the truth that God is my defender, I respond with mercy. In both cases, my behaviors reveal their source. Jesus never reacted. He only responded to His Father's truth.

REFLECTION QUESTION: Think of a time when you reacted in a way you regret. What does it tell you about your thinking?

_____
_____
_____
_____
_____

It's time to occupy God's promises for you!

If you are tired of running from the same giants, going around the mountain, or coming up short of your breakthrough, then you're ready to get unstuck. It's time to break camp, pack up, and move on! Moses continues in Deuteronomy 1:21, "*Look! He has placed the land in front of you. Go and occupy it as the* L ORD, *the God of your ancestors, has promised you. Don't be afraid! Don't be discouraged!*'"

Chapter 8: Determine Your Commitment

The Israelites had hundreds of years of mistreatment in Egypt. They had physically left the land and slavery, but their mindset was stuck in the past. God wasn't just asking them to leave behind the place where they were camped. He was asking them to leave behind old mindsets. God knew those old mindsets would cause fear to rise up in them when they got to Canaan. Those slave mindsets helped them survive in Egypt but would stifle them in Canaan. We, too, have mindsets that have helped us survive in past seasons but will stifle us in future ones.

The fact that Moses tells the people not to be afraid or discouraged makes it clear that crossing the threshold would not be easy. It would demand greater levels of trust than ever before. Yes, God wanted to give them this land, but more importantly, God wanted them to experience Him in ways they never had before. There are aspects of God you can only experience when you step out in faith. You can know God's promises and stay where you are, but you cannot experience the God of Promise unless you leave camp. The Israelites had His promises all along. It wasn't until they finally crossed into Canaan that they experienced Him as the God of Promise! No matter how great the promise is, the Promiser is even better!

REFLECTION QUESTION: What has God placed in front of you to occupy?

_____
_____
_____
_____
_____

So, what will you be most committed to?

I have a rule that every time I go shopping, I get rid of a shirt for every new shirt I buy. The same thing goes for sweaters, pants, and even sweatshirts. This rule is harder to implement than it sounds, for when it's time to decide which items need to go, I'm hesitant to let anything go. What if I regret my choice? What if a month from now I wish I had that shirt back? This is known as the fear of loss. It describes an irrational fear we have in giving something up in order to have something new.

Fear of loss keeps us stuck. Consider the wife who stays in an abusive marriage because she's afraid of what she might lose. If she walks away now, she might miss out on the chance that he'll change. If she walks away now, will it make all of her tears and effort worthless? Or what if no one else will love her and she misses out on the chance to have companionship again? The fear of losing those things "justifies" staying in the abuse. Or how about the person who stays to work for an unethical boss because they have invested years in the company? To leave now would mean losing all they have worked for and starting fresh elsewhere. To leave now would be losing the comfort of routine and relationships with co-workers. The fear of losing those things "justifies" staying in an unethical situation. These examples show how our desire to avoid loss comes at the expense of what we might gain by letting go.

The Israelites had to leave something behind in order to go forward. They liked Mount Sinai and had no guarantee they would like Canaan more. We cannot cross our threshold and move into something new without being willing to leave something behind. It was a risk to go forward. They had to cross into the unknown and unfamiliar. They had a promise, but attaining the promise would require trust. I assure you, God never asks you to move on without offering you the promise of something better.

Chapter 8: Determine Your Commitment

Each lie you believe has served a purpose, but it has cost you far more than you realize. You've reached a point of decision. What are you going to be most committed to? Is it the mindset that got you stuck, or are you ready to commit to a new way of thinking?

REFLECTION QUESTION: I am most committed to: _____ _____.

CHAPTER 9

FIND THE TRUTH

Consider how different these strategies are: Satan presents a distorted version of the truth so he can steal from you. God presents a clear version of the truth so He can give to you. Vastly different strategies to serve very different motives. God wants to make the lies plain and visible in your life so you can deal with them and exchange them for truth. He does this so you can be free. Psalm 119:130 says, "*The teaching of your word gives light, so even the simple can understand.*" Real truth isn't complicated; it's quite simple and accessible. However, simple doesn't mean shallow or easy. He gives truth, but we still have to discover it.

Hebrews 4:12 describes truth as "*...alive and powerful. It is sharper than the sharpest two-edged sword, cutting between soul and spirit, between joint and marrow. It exposes our innermost thoughts and desires.*" Only God's Word can pierce the tangled mess of our soul to separate truth from lie. He doesn't do this to bring more chaos to the mess, but to bring clarity to the mess.

So far, we've defined stronghold as a place where a particular belief has a "strong hold" on your life, producing negative effects. But there is a redemptive definition for the word as well. A stronghold can also be a place that is built up and well-established to protect against an attack, like a fortress. We see this in Psalms 9:9, which says the Lord is a stronghold, or secure place, in times of trouble. When lies establish a stronghold in our thoughts, we become captive to those lies. When truth establishes a stronghold, our mind is protected against the mental attacks of the enemy.

It is not a question as to whether we will have strongholds in our minds, but rather which type of stronghold they will be. This decision determines which portion of John 10:10 our lives will reflect. The fruit of a lie is *"to steal and kill and destroy,"* but the fruit of truth is *"a rich and satisfying life."*

Deconstructing the lie

Satan constructs his lies with a predictable process. After all, he stole the idea of process from God and then twisted it for his own kingdom! There's a popular food trend right now where restaurants offer "deconstructed food." Elements of a dish that are typically combined and presented in a certain way, like a sandwich, are broken apart and served separately in a creative manner. Each component is treated individually instead of becoming a lost ingredient in the dish. While I enjoy a good deconstructed sandwich as much as anyone, I enjoy deconstructing lies even more! To dismantle the enemy's lies, we'll break apart the different components of his lie-building process and address them individually.

To reverse the lie, we will start with what is seen above the surface and work our way to the root.

DECONSTRUCTING A LIE

STEP 1	EXAMINE RESULTS	What results am I getting? What behaviors cause those results?
STEP 2	IDENTIFY THE STRONGHOLD	What lie do I believe that steers those behaviors and results?
STEP 3	BREAK YOUR AGREEMENT	In what ways have I come into agreement with this lie?
STEP 4	UPROOT THE LIE	Where did this lie first emerge in my thinking (event)?
STEP 5	IDENTIFY THE TRUTH	How is this lie a distortion of what really happened?
STEP 6	GET GOD'S TRUTH	What is the seed of truth in the event? What is God's truth about that truth?

We deconstruct each step in the process until we arrive at the original truth that holds the entire lie together and is the basis for the lie's credibility. Without it, the lie falls apart. When a lie is tangled with the truth, it's much like a pile of jumbled Christmas lights—you can't tell one part of the strand from the next. Since Satan starts with the truth, you want to find the starting point the same way you find the beginning of the strand of lights so you can untangle the pile.

Activity: Deconstructing a Lie

1. What area of my life is not producing the results I desire?
_____
_____

_____
_____

2. What behavior produces or contributes to those results?
_____
_____
_____
_____

3. What lie drives that behavior?
_____
_____
_____
_____

4. In what ways have I come into agreement with this lie?
_____
_____
_____
_____

5. Where did this lie first emerge in my thinking (event)?
_____
_____
_____
_____

6. How is that lie a distortion of the truth?
_____
_____
_____

7. What is the truth in the lie?
_____
_____
_____
_____

Get to the core lie

Several years ago, my mom purchased an old dresser at an estate sale. This piece of antique furniture had accumulated many coats of paint over the years. Each layer of paint had to be painstakingly removed until the original wood grain was exposed and could be restored to its original condition. Those layers were messy and ugly—the exact opposite of the finished result. If she had aborted the project mid-process, she would have aborted the end result. There will be times your process feels exhausting and overwhelming. And in those moments, the Holy Spirit will beckon you to keep going. Where He is leading you is worth the price of the journey.

We previously learned how the enemy layers lies upon lies to create a snowball effect. For this reason, each layer reveals a new lie that must be unburied and addressed. This is true of any ungodly stronghold in your life. It is a series of interdependent, layered lies that must be systematically deconstructed. It looks much like a game of Jenga®—each block that is removed brings the tower closer to toppling down. In Jenga, the goal is to keep the tower standing, but in removing mental strongholds, the goal is to remove the blocks one by one until the stronghold falls. It becomes more unstable with each block removed, and as the stronghold loses its power, you experience new freedom that spurs you on to the next step.

For most people, deconstructing one lie will lead to the realization that deeper ones still exist. Part of staying with the process is allowing the Holy Spirit to go deeper until you get to the core lie—the root of your faulty belief system. You identify a thistle by what you see above the ground, but you remove it by dealing with the root under the surface. If you only mow off the top, it will grow back.

So, how can you know you've truly found the root of a lie, especially when there are layers to the lies you believe? How can you know the lie won't eventually grow back? All beliefs stem from your beliefs about who God is or is not. When you get to the lie about God's nature, you can know you've reached the core lie and can destroy the root.

> ### Margot's Story: Stuck in Self-sabotage
>
> Margot struggled with her weight for many years. After experiencing some significant results with a healthy eating and exercise plan, she fell off the wagon and gained the weight back. This wasn't the first time; it was a pattern of sabotaging her own success. The discouragement and shame from another failure felt overwhelming. She was stuck and ready to give up.
>
> She believed several lies about her ability to lose weight and keep it off. She was convinced she wouldn't be able to break free from the pattern, that she would continue to fail, and that she wasn't disciplined enough to stick with it. Ironically, these beliefs produced her cyclical failures. She was aware of these lies and had done her best to convince herself otherwise. But they held a grip on her because they were attached to deeper lies.
>
> As she sought the Lord, He began to show her the deeper lies. She believed there was something inherently wrong with her that would always prevent

> her from having success—not just with her weight but also with her marriage, parenting, career, and faith. This lie told her she wasn't capable of success and wasn't worthy of it either. This stronghold permeated her life, causing her to self-destruct in many ways.
>
> And yet, these lies kept their grip because of an even deeper lie. Buried beneath those lies was the core lie that fueled everything. She believed God had messed up when He made her, and therefore, He was not trustworthy. If He made a mistake, how could He be trusted with anything? What looked like an issue of weight on the surface was an issue of trust at the core.

The core lie of all deceit is that you can't trust God. This was true for Adam and Eve and was true for Margot. While all of those lies affected her, it was the deepest lie that supported the others. The Holy Spirit exposed that core lie and ministered the truth to Margot that she was, in fact, fearfully and wonderfully made. It was this truth about His work and her worth that allowed her to break free from all the other lies, too.

GOING EVEN DEEPER

```
┌─────────────────────────────────────────────────┐
│                    RESULTS                      │
│  ─────────────────────────────────────────────  │
│                   BEHAVIORS                     │
│  ─────────────────────────────────────────────  │
│                                                 │
│                    FEELINGS                     │
│                                                 │
│  ─────────────────────────────────────────────  │
│  Surface lie                      Surface truth │
│                                                 │
│  Lie about you      THOUGHTS      Truth about you│
│                                                 │
│  Core lie about God          Core truth about God│
└─────────────────────────────────────────────────┘
```

Get close to your pain

Part of what makes it so difficult to peel back layers of lies is that they are often covering pain. Since lies start with an event or an experience, it is likely you will need to get close to your pain to find the truth. This goes against our grain, as we spend much of our lives trying to avoid pain!

Because pain is hard for us to process, it often gets buried below the surface, unresolved. The pain we feel is real, even if the thought process behind the pain is misleading. We often use our pain as validation for the lies we believe about our situations. Sometimes, pain is the only thing we take away from the situation, so it serves as proof of what happened to us. In this way, we carry pain like a battle wound. The pain we keep and the lies we believe maintain a symbiotic relationship. The lie protects the pain, and the unresolved pain protects the lie. For this reason, we cannot uproot lies without uncovering our pain.

> ### Sharon's Story: Stuck in Pain
>
> After several years of extremely painful estrangement with a close family member, the person had a change of heart and their relationship was restored. This was an answer to years of Sharon's prayers, diligent forgiveness, and releasing her expectations to God. It was wonderful! What she wasn't prepared for was the unexpected anger that resurfaced soon after reconciliation. Sure, things were good now, but what about the years of sadness and all the time that was lost? She had worked hard to keep that pain at bay for years just so she could cope and continue living life. Though she had forgiven, the thought of fully moving on felt like her years of pain counted for nothing. Her attachment to pain was meeting a need because it validated her hurt and gave meaning to her struggles.
>
> Sharon chose to get close to her pain. She brought this fear that her pain didn't matter before the Lord. He asked her to trust Him with the part of her heart that was still wounded. She said, "Yes, I trust You with my heart" and surrendered it to Him. Within a few days, the anger was gone and there was a deep healing happening in her heart. It allowed her to fully embrace God's restorative work and find joy in the relationship again.

Pain kept in the dark manifests in every area of your life, whether you know it or not. Unfinished business can cause great damage to you and those around you. Avoidance never brings healing. In fact, we repeat what doesn't get healed. The way we get healed and break free from patterns is to uncover and expose our pain to the love of Christ. It's much like when you're driving down the street looking for the street sign of your next turn. You can see signs from afar and squint to try to read them, but it isn't until you get up close that you can identify the street with certainty. In the same way, we have to get close to our pain to identify it and receive healing in that place. When you find the place of pain and allow Jesus into that place, the root of the lie will lose its hold on you. We must get close to it so He can get close to it.

How do you uncover your pain and expose it to the love of Christ? It starts by asking the Holy Spirit to reveal the source of your pain and the source of the lie. He will gently bring to your remembrance an event or an experience. Many times these have been forgotten or seemingly insignificant experiences! When He reveals this place of hurt, He will neutralize that pain by giving you a new perspective on what happened or by showing you His presence in that situation.

> ### Marie's Story: Stuck in Fear
>
> Marie grew up in a poor family with alcoholism and all the dysfunctions that come with it. In her late 30s, her in-laws were setting up their estate plan and rewriting their will. Marie and her husband worked with them in the family business along with their teenage children. Since the business was the primary source of income for Marie's family, they needed to know how to plan for the future. However, her in-laws were secretive about their plans. She knew the will was their choice and there was nothing she could do to control the process. This caused her a lot of stress and anxiety.

> She struggled with it for months and no matter what she told herself, it bothered her. She couldn't shake it. She had prayed about it many times, but nothing changed. One night when it was weighing heavily on her, she cried out to God and begged Him to show her how to move past it. She quieted herself and just listened to hear what He might say. When she did, He revealed the layers of lies fueling her anxiety.
>
> The initial layer of lies was that her family wouldn't have their needs met if the will wasn't written fairly. Underneath that layer, God showed her she was afraid she would die with no one to take care of her. This fear stemmed from a childhood where she worried each day about whether her needs would be met. But deep below the surface was a lie that God wasn't going to take care of her—that she would be left to take care of herself like she did as a child. This lie was rooted in pain from her childhood. When He revealed this to her, she saw how this pain had driven her to self-sufficiency. She said out loud, "I'm sorry for not trusting You." Immediately, the fear that was the root of her stress and anxiety left and never came back. God began a process of bringing deep healing to her, uprooting the lies of abandonment and poverty in her life.

Receiving healing for your pain doesn't erase the memory of what happened or negate the wrong done to you, but it does neutralize the experience. I cut my finger while doing yard work this year. The wound was deep enough that it took several days to heal and significant enough that it left me with a scar. That scar is a record the wound occurred, but it doesn't have the power to hurt me anymore. When God neutralizes our pain, He takes away that event's power to hurt us any further. It takes away the sting so it no longer steers your life from under the surface. And most importantly, it neutralizes the lie that was born in that painful moment.

We often mistake our numbness to pain as healing. If you sit on your foot long enough, it will become numb. Your heart works the same way. Numbness is not healing, but neutralization is. When you can think about the event that happened and feel neutral about what occurred, you have received healing in that place.

I recommend using a tool to get close to your pain. Here are three tools I've found effective:

1. **Counseling** – Counselors are skilled at helping you get close to your pain, exposing lies, and identifying thresholds. It gives you a safe place to explore hurtful events, gain an understanding of how those events affect you, and find a sense of closure for your pain. For me, counseling has provided the necessary clarity and guidance needed to speed up my healing process.

2. **Journaling** – Writing down our emotions and thoughts can be a powerful way to uncover beliefs and discover the truth. The reflection questions included in this book are a great starting point for journaling. I would also encourage you to pause while journaling to give the Holy Spirit an opportunity to speak to what you've written. Ask Him, "What do You want me to know about this?" His answers will always help you heal.

3. **Mind-mapping** – This tool creates a visual map of how different events and experiences contribute to and are connected with the lies you believe. Here's an example:

Chapter 9: Find the Truth

MIND-MAP OF LIES

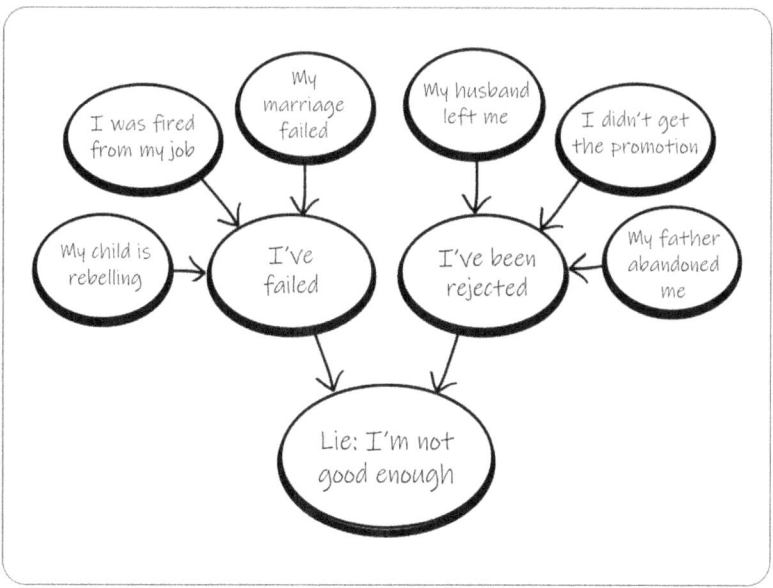

You can see from this simple mind map that many experiences may fuel one lie, and more than one lie may fuel a deeper lie. We could continue to map out the lies and relationships until we get to the core. There's something about putting it on paper that makes it less intimidating and easier to untangle the experiences and lies.

Get God's truth about your truth

Once you find the seed of truth, you will find that the Holy Spirit longs to give you revelation about that original element of truth. If the enemy's commentary sought to bring destruction in your life, the Holy Spirit's commentary brings life! Remember, truth begets truth, and the truth about your truth will bring great freedom. Let's revisit some examples from this book to see how God speaks truth to the element of truth:

IDENTIFYING GOD'S TRUTH

ADAM AND EVE
The lie: God doesn't want us to eat from the tree, so He's not trustworthy.
The truth: We can't eat from the tree.
God's truth about the truth: We can't eat from the tree, but it is because God loves us and is protecting us.

REBECCA
The lie: I must strive to be good enough so I can please others.
The truth: I'm afraid I won't be good enough to please God and others.
God's truth about the truth: I can't please everyone, but God delights in me, exactly as I am.

ELIZABETH
The lie: I didn't have the answer, so I'm not smart.
The truth: I didn't have the answer to the math problem.
God's truth about the truth: I didn't have the answer at that moment, but God gave me the exact intelligence and talents I need.

SHARON
The lie: If I let go of my pain, it will be wasted.
The truth: I'm wounded by a relationship.
God's truth about the truth: I'm wounded, but I can trust God with those wounds.

MARY
The lie: If the will isn't fair, no one will take care of me.
The truth: My needs weren't met like they should have been, so I was fearful.
God's truth about the truth: My needs weren't met like they should have been, but I can trust God to take care of me.

God led me through a process of dealing with my shame when He peeled back what I thought I believed about myself to expose what I truly believed about myself. It was both an incredibly painful and incredibly freeing process. In many ways, it felt like the Lord performed surgery on my heart, using a two-edged scalpel with perfect precision and care. And yet again, His wounds were for my healing and my good.

Amid seeing these hard things, He gave me another vision to speak truth to my lies. I saw two distinct lists: One of the lists was significantly longer than the other, to the point it had so many items listed on it that I was unable to focus on any one item in particular. This long list represented all the reasons why God shouldn't love and pursue me. It detailed failures, weaknesses, things I hate about myself, and even things that others find irritating about me. In contrast, the shortlist only had one item on it. It said, "I am worthy." It was clear as day and jumped off the page at me. My list was full of limiting beliefs, but His list was a liberating belief. How freeing it is to know that His belief defines me—all I must do is come into agreement with it! In fact, His belief about my worth makes my long list irrelevant. If you let Him, He will help you peel away the lies one by one so you can embrace His truth, too. It's worth going under the scalpel to experience the love of the Surgeon.

> ### Breann's Story: Stuck in Guilt
>
> Breann carried guilt about her grandfather's recent death. He had passed away unexpectedly and alone, with no one there to say goodbye. She had been closer to her grandfather than her own parents, so his passing had a profound effect on her. Because she hadn't said goodbye or been present when he passed, she believed she had failed him. Not only was the guilt weighing her down, but it was preventing her from working through grief in a healthy way.
>
> In a conversation with a friend, Breann shared how she could never forgive herself for not being there when he died. After all, she was supposed to stop by the night he died but had made other plans. As she spoke, she began to realize she had bought into a lie.
>
> The friend asked, "Out of everything you just shared with me, what do you know is positively true?" The truth of the situation was that her grandpa had died

> and she had not been there. The friend pressed further, "Now what would Jesus say to you about that truth?" She closed her eyes and took a few breaths. "Jesus says He will never leave me and there's nothing I can do or not do to make Him leave me."
>
> On the surface, she believed the lie that it was her fault. Beneath that was a lie that her grandpa had abandoned her. And beneath that was a lie that God might do the same. In one moment and one simple sentence, Jesus pierced through layers of lies to get to the core. She had gained heaven's perspective and it neutralized the lies. Peace washed over Breann and her grieving process finally began.

To understand the importance of infusing God's perspective into your situation, I want to look at how another man in the Bible, Asaph, relied on God to get unstuck. Psalm 73 is one of my favorite chapters of the Bible. I admire how raw and real Asaph is in his writing. He isn't afraid to show us just how human he is, which makes him easy to relate to.

Asaph was a well-educated man and was the head worship leader. He had spent years studying God and knew all about His nature. Despite what he knew from his education, he gets stuck in his thoughts and gets mad at God, which just goes to show that no one is exempt from getting stuck. It doesn't matter how spiritual, educated, or smart you are.

Asaph begins in verses 1–4, "*Truly God is good to Israel, to those whose hearts are pure. But as for me, I almost lost my footing. My feet were slipping, and I was almost gone. For I envied the proud when I saw them prosper despite their wickedness. They seem to live such painless lives; their bodies are so healthy and strong. They don't have troubles like other people; they're not plagued with problems like everyone else.*" He is confident that God is good. The use of the word "truly" to start off denotes an assertive statement of truth. To say that God is good is to say the sum of all His qualities is good, through and through. If you were to dissect all the characteristics of God, you wouldn't find any part of Him that is not good. And yet, Asaph sees something in his life that feels contrary to that truth. It is a crisis of faith. If God is truly good, through and through, why does He seem to be good to those who don't deserve it, while overlooking Asaph? Surely a good God would be fairer than that?

Asaph's struggle is with what seems to be happening, and that is true for you and me as well. He believes God is good and has a clear idea of what HE thinks that should look like. In this case, Asaph's interpretation of God's goodness is that it always translates to earthly blessings. This is his belief framework for interpreting his experiences, and what he saw contradicted his conviction. He saw wicked people prospering (an element of truth) and thought he was getting the raw end of the deal (a lie).

The biggest threat to our belief in God's goodness is our sense of fairness. The enemy wants you to doubt God's fairness by distracting you with what seems to be true. This is the same trick he used on Eve! Asaph is consumed by the supposed prosperity of the wickedness. He was angry by what he saw, and he believed he was being treated unfairly. Your feelings and your behaviors follow your focus.

Have you ever noticed when you are riding a bike and look to your right that your bike tends to veer to the right? It is the same with our focus. We veer to the place of our focus. Eve's focus switched from the presence of God to the presence of that tree, and her behavior followed. If our focus is on believing God is treating others better than He treats us, then our behavior will veer towards that. We become angry at God and jealous of others.

Asaph's perception almost caused him to lose his footing. The enemy wants you to stumble, so he seeks to create a conflict in your thoughts between what you believe and what you are experiencing. And just as he did with Eve, if he can get you to question what you are experiencing, He can get you to question God's fairness. If he can get you to question God's fairness, he can get you to question God's trustworthiness. And if he can get you to question God's trustworthiness, he can get you to question the value of your obedience.

I can relate to Asaph in many ways. Life isn't playing out like he expected, causing him to grapple with his beliefs. You've likely been there. He's devoted his entire life to serving God, and his expectations of God aren't being met. Surely life should be easier for those serving God than for those who don't!

This crisis of faith comes amid great disappointment, to the point he begins to question the purpose of his obedience. He wonders in verses 13–14, *"Did I keep my heart pure for nothing? Did I keep myself innocent for no reason? I get nothing but trouble all day long; every morning brings me pain."* A lie begins to take root: God is unfair, therefore my obedience doesn't matter.

So, what does Asaph do with this lie? He takes it into his time with God. Verses 16–17 continues, *"So I tried to understand why the wicked prosper. But what a difficult task it is! Then I went into your sanctuary, O God, and I finally understood the destiny of the wicked."* Asaph's perspective changed when he entered into the presence of God. Every time you encounter the presence of God, you encounter truth. For Asaph and for us, an earthly perspective will never provide the power to be free from lies. This is why His presence is transforming in nature and why we cannot expect to live transformed lives without a daily commitment to abide in His presence. Intimacy is the source of truth that sets you free, not knowledge.

I have a co-worker who recently finished a complete remodel of her house. The house was gutted down to the studs and completely rebuilt. One of the final steps in this lengthy process was painting the bedrooms. She selected a soft gray paint. After the contractor was done painting the bedrooms, she stopped by to see the progress. What she didn't anticipate was how the natural light of the one bedroom in the front of the house would affect the way the paint looked. All the bedrooms looked soft gray, except this one. It looked like a light blue. The paint was the same, but the light changed how the paint appeared to the eye. This is what truth does for our situations. The situations may remain the same, but the light of truth causes us to see the situation differently.

We have a tendency to judge God's work based on the season or the circumstance we are in, rather than seeing the entirety (or the eternity) of it. If you take any complicated process in business and look at a small sliver, that part of the process will likely not make sense. "Sense making" comes from this context: what comes before in the process, what comes after in the process, and the desired end result. Without this context, the sliver of the process has no purpose or meaning. The same is true in our lives. We look at an event in our lives as a complete story when it's actually only a chapter of God's plan and purpose for us. It's only when we gain heaven's context that the chapter takes on meaning and importance in our lives. God's work may not appear to be fair in the short-term, but it is always just in the long-term.

Asaph knew about God's goodness before this, but he truly EXPERIENCED God's goodness in this moment of honesty.

The enemy's lies work to get us distracted or discouraged from entering into God's presence. Every time you spend time with God, it's an opportunity for you to gain a new perspective, new understanding, new truth. Be with God. Be angry. Be sad. Be hurt. God's not afraid of your wrestling or emotion. Being authentic about why you're hurting is a beautiful part of the surrender process. Asaph's struggle was about to produce a revelation; your struggle will do the same.

"*He declares, 'Whom have I in heaven but you? I desire you more than anything on earth. My health may fail, and my spirit may grow weak, but God remains the strength of my heart; he is mine forever'*" (Psalm 73:25–26). Talk about a transformation of emotions! To read that chapter at first blush, you might think Asaph is moody and can't make up his mind about how he feels. But instead, it shows us how truth interrupts our errant thought processes and overhauls our thinking! Asaph's new perspective is accompanied by new emotions of hope and gratitude. He concludes with this thought: "*But as for me, how good it is to be near God! I have made the Sovereign Lord my shelter, and I will tell everyone about the wonderful things you do.*" Asaph found truth, and the truth set him free.

ASAPH DISCOVERS GOD'S TRUTH

ASAPH

The lie: My obedience doesn't matter, so I should just stop trying.
The truth: Wicked people appear to be prospering. It doesn't seem fair.
God's truth about the truth: Wicked people appear to be prospering, but my relationship with God is the greatest treasure. When I focus on this truth, that's all that matters!

Agreement with Truth

If we underestimate the power of our agreement with a lie, then we vastly underestimate the power of our agreement with truth. A person who agrees with the truth will end up living a life that aligns with truth because agreement leads to alignment. And yet, we very rarely speak about the intentionality of agreeing with truth. It's much more than mental assent, but instead is a shift of lordship.

I want to walk you through what this has looked like for me. I've identified five clear stages of the process, each one leading to the next. Agreement with truth is just the beginning of the establishment of truth in that area of your life. It's like laying a foundation, which you build upon until you have a solid framework of truth within your thoughts. But as with any new build, getting the foundation right is of utmost importance.

THE FIVE STAGES OF AGREEING WITH TRUTH

STAGE ONE: Repent for Believing the Lie
STAGE TWO: Renounce the Lie
STAGE THREE: Identify the Truth
STAGE FOUR: Declare the Truth
STAGE FIVE: Submit to the Truth

Transformation begins with **repentance**. Repentance makes room for truth to make its home in you. When we talk about repentance, it is generally in the context of turning from our sins. This is a Biblically accurate representation but not a full one. Certainly, repentance does mean to turn from sin and move in the opposite direction, but more specifically, it is when we evict the lie we believe and make room for truth in our lives.

We vastly undervalue the benefits of repentance. For starters, a major reason that believers don't understand the love of God is that they don't understand repentance. It's the kindness of the Lord that leads us to repentance (Romans 2:4), and it's in repentance that we experience how good, kind, loving, and merciful He truly is. The more I make repentance a normal part of my life, the more experiencing His love becomes a normal part of my life. Nothing gets you unstuck like experiencing God's love.

Isaiah 57:15 says He will restore the crushed spirit of the humble and revive the courage of those with repentant hearts. I love the way The Message paraphrases this verse in this way, "*I live with the high and holy places, but also with the low-spirited, the spirit-crushed. And what I do is put a new spirit in them, get them up on their feet again.*" Repentance restores our lives from the inside out and is an important step in the healing process, as it removes the power of shame to continually dredge up our shortcomings. A person who is crushed by the weight of their sin and bondage is hunched over, defeated, with their eyes looking down. Repentance restores that person to an upright stance by removing the burden of sin, shame, and failure.

An often overlooked aspect of repentance is that it brings you closure. It allows you to receive and accept forgiveness from the Lord and move forward. It dislodges us from regret and shame and is a natural way God gives us closure for the past. Just feeling remorseful isn't the same as repentance, and it leaves the door open to shame and to the enemy, which is why it leaves us stuck. Remorse is feeling bad for what you've done without taking responsibility to change. Repentance closes the door on what happened to you and to what you did. That closure is not only for you but also to keep the enemy from taking back territory.

Even when we are wronged, our repentance is part of discovering truth. We are responsible to repent for any thoughts or responses we have that aren't aligned with truth. There is no degree of injury inflicted upon us that will ever excuse us from being responsible for our thought-lives. This step of repentance moves us out of victimhood and into a place of ownership, where we can clearly see any contributions we've made to the situation.

PRAYER POINT: *"Jesus, I repent for being stuck. I repent for believing the lie that _____. I confess I have been more committed to _____ than I have been trusting You. I ask Your forgiveness for my sin and the pride in my heart. I know Your blood was shed for my sins and that I've been washed whiter than snow. There is no shame or condemnation for me, only Your love and mercy. Because of those things, I can come boldly before You and ask You to do a powerful work in my life. I close the door on those past thoughts and behaviors and step into what You've called me to become. I ask You to transform my mind and my life so I am aligned with Your will. In Jesus's Name, Amen."*

Second, you must **renounce the lie**. Before we can agree with the truth, we must disagree with the lie. We must break up with the lies that have entangled us, served as idols, and robbed us of abundant life. We must say to the devil, "It's not me; it's you—and I refuse to believe the lie you are selling me any longer!" The moment you begin to reject the lie the enemy has been selling, you begin to walk in the freedom that was purchased for you. We must reject the counterfeit to embrace the real.

I consider myself to be a great dog parent, and I like to splurge on fun toys for my dogs. When Sadie was younger, she had a surplus of toys to pick from, and yet she insisted on carrying around this ugly stuffed rabbit toy. It was hideous enough to scare a small child and large enough to make it hard for Sadie to handle—to the point that she had a hard time seeing around it. And yet, she loved that thing and carried it from room to room with her. She had better options for toys and companions, but she couldn't pick them up until she put down the rabbit she was attached to. We can't pick up the truth until we relinquish the lies we're attached to.

If the lie gained power through your agreement, it loses its power through your disagreement. Renouncement is ending your agreement with a lie and beginning a new agreement with truth. Since it is an agreement, I believe it is important to renounce it out loud.

PRAYER POINT: *"Jesus, I renounce this lie in my life and no longer give it a place to rule over me. By the power of Your blood, I break off that lie's assignment against me to steal, kill, and destroy me. Holy Spirit, I ask You to reveal the truth that longs to make its home in me and bring You abundant life."*

Next, you **identify the truth**. I have a small area of my yard that is resistant to grass for no apparent reason. After trying different varieties of grass, the previous owner eventually found success with a very resilient form of grass called zoysia. The secret to this variety's success is that it is so thick and dense, it doesn't allow room for any weeds to take root and grow. It's also highly resistant to drought and heat. On the other hand, typical grass seed like Kentucky bluegrass has a much shallower root system and can be easily overtaken by the presence of more dominant weeds. One of the primary ways you can tell my yard has two types of grass is that the zoysia doesn't have dandelions, while the Kentucky bluegrass is full of them!

Chapter 9: Find the Truth

Lies are like weeds. In the absence of truth, they will fill your heart and mind. Just as healthy grass starves weeds, giving them no place to grow, minds that are full of truth starve out lies. We are each responsible for filling ourselves with truth, which is why daily time reading the Word is important. It creates weed-resistant soil in your heart. It also teaches you how to spot lies. It's easy to spot a weed in the middle of a healthy lawn because it sticks out like a sore thumb, but a weed in the middle of a weed patch just blends in. What does the Bible have to say about the lie you believe? What truth does it offer in its place?

For what God wants to do in and through you, He must weed out the lies. Carnal thinking cannot support Kingdom activity, and He will use any circumstance He can to surface and starve a lie. It's part of His loving nature. Colossians 3:1–2 says, *"Since you have been raised to new life with Christ, set your sights on the realities of heaven, where Christ sits in the place of honor at God's right hand. Think about the things of heaven, not the things of earth."* Faith is seeing things God's way. It is submitting to God's reality rather than choosing my version over His.

After you've identified it, you **declare truth**. Confession has to do with repenting for what you've previously believed, but declaration has to do with what you now choose to believe. During an intensely painful situation where close friends had severely betrayed me, the Lord instructed me to sing the old song "God Is So Good" to the wounded parts of my heart until my heart began to sing it back. It sounds silly, but I did it. In my pain, I didn't always *feel* like God was good, but I was scattering seeds of truth over my pain so it could take root in those parts of my soul. Over time, I began to see how the truth of His goodness began to mend my crushed heart and overtake the lies that sought to keep me angry and wounded. I'm not suggesting we talk at our pain to suppress or ignore it. Instead, I'm suggesting we invite His truth into those moments of pain so He can begin to transform our thoughts and emotions.

Let me give you some more practical examples of what this might look like for you. You can speak to the rejected parts of your heart with His truth about how much He loves you. Remind the broken parts of your heart about His ability to comfort. Where there is unforgiveness, speak to your heart to release and forgive just as you have been forgiven. In addition, find Scriptures that speak light to the dark truth you believe. When you feel fear, speak to your fear and say, "Your truth says You have not given me a spirit of fear but a spirit of love and a sound mind. I refuse to submit my will to fear, and instead, I submit my will to Your truth." If you have believed the lie of shame, find verses that talk about your identity in Christ. In doing so, you allow the truth to establish godly strongholds within your thoughts.

We previously discussed that emotions are the result of our thinking. Cyclical thinking results in cyclical feelings, behaviors, and results. When we renew our mind with the Word, our heart (also called our soul, which is the place of our emotions) becomes convinced of the truth. Our emotions will follow our truth. Speaking truth is not dismissing our emotions, but rather reshaping our thinking so our emotions can be transformed. I didn't *feel* like God was good at first, but eventually, my emotions followed the truth I was speaking (or, in my case, singing!). I was able to change my feelings, behaviors, and results by changing my thinking.

Finally, you must **submit to that truth**. We choose whether we submit to a lie or submit to truth. There's a verse in 1 Peter 1:22 that says, "*You were cleansed from your sins when you obeyed the truth.*" The word "obeyed" means submitted. Obedience isn't a begrudging or reluctant act of compliance. Obedience happens when we submit our thoughts and our emotions to the truth. As we submit our thoughts and emotions to the truth, there is a cleansing that happens inwardly and is expressed outwardly.

Sometimes obedience just seems too hard—we've tried and failed too many times, or it feels like it's beyond our ability. God told the Israelites in Isaiah 1:19, *"If you are willing and obedient, you will eat the good of the land."* The word "willing" carries the implication of *being willing to be willing*. If obedience seems overwhelming, just start by being willing to let the Holy Spirit make you willing. God can do a whole lot with just a little bit of willingness.

I guarantee the enemy will do his best to orchestrate a situation to make it appear your new truth is failing you. These are the times when you must set your face like flint (Isaiah 50:7) and commit yourself wholeheartedly to truth and obedience to that truth. As you submit to truth, you establish that new truth in your thinking, and, in the process, the old lie will lose its influence over you. The more you submit to the truth, the more freedom you will experience.

PRAYER POINT: *"The truth is _____. I choose to submit my thinking, my emotions, and my behavior to this truth. I will learn to walk out this truth every single day, with Your guidance, Holy Spirit. Thank you for leading me in this truth and setting me free!"*

CHAPTER 10

ACT WITH COURAGE

Redefining courage

One thing is for sure: Doing nothing is the surefire way to remain stuck. The behaviors that got you stuck won't get you unstuck. To break out of cyclical behaviors, you must behave in a different way, one that feels unfamiliar and even scary. For this reason, getting unstuck requires a new level of trust in God. This is why it is so crucial you get to the core lie that He is untrustworthy. You get unstuck by realizing He is trustworthy and then acting like it! It means stepping out in your new truth, even if it doesn't feel true yet. The Israelites finally trusted God would give them the victory over the giants, even though the giants were still there. They still felt fear; they just chose to trust anyway.

Courage is doing something that has an element of uncertainty about it. According to this definition, driving to work requires courage! Uncertainty is a precursor for progress. If you want to cross over your threshold, you must embrace the uncertainty that is to come. That's where the trust comes in. Truth requires action. For it to produce benefits in your life, it has to become an ongoing practice.

Even though our behaviors are the results of our thoughts, sometimes we need to intentionally choose new actions to initiate new patterns. These actions can serve as a catalyst for change in our thinking. Here are 10 ideas for courageous acts that can help you get started:

10 Acts of Courage

1. Articulate what you want.

The fact that you feel stuck is evidence that you were created for more than this. That stirring within you isn't just wrestling with your current circumstances, but instead a desire for your future to emerge. It's evidence you're ready for what comes next.

If you ask most adults what they want, they won't be able to tell you. They can barely tell you what they want for dinner, let alone what they want in life. The question "what do you want?" feels risky because it threatens our status quo. As adults, we have experienced great disappointment. We have learned that we can't have what we want, and we've learned that things don't always work out the way we want. We've learned dreaming isn't a "responsible" thing to do. Because of those experiences, we avoid answering the question.

I'm often called upon to mentor young leaders who have come to a point in their career where they feel torn and must decide about which path to take. It never fails that when I ask the question "What do you want?" it stops them in their tracks. It interrupts their brains, and it engages their hearts. You see, your real answer to the question "what do you want?" is almost always about purpose and destiny. It's rarely about logic and lists.

I suspect there are many of us who are afraid to answer the question "what do I want," because then we must face the consequences of what we already know to be true. Maybe the consequence is disappointing a parent. Perhaps the result is that I'll have to act upon what I want—and owning it feels far scarier than denying it. Maybe it hurts too much to hope for something different than what we have. It's a risk to define and articulate what we want. Unfortunately, not taking that risk comes at a great expense. A life without purpose or with misplaced purpose isn't living. It's merely existing.

Others never answer the question for themselves but allow another person to answer it for them. Letting another person define your purpose for you will result in you becoming stuck. The short-term payoff is acceptance and approval. The long-term cost is forfeiture of your purpose and potential. In essence, it's forfeiture of God's design for your life. These people suppress their purpose in exchange for pleasing others, and in the process, they lose themselves entirely. If you find yourself stuck today, it may be because you've lost yourself somewhere along the way. The good news is that it doesn't make you lost altogether. You are just stuck. And that makes you a perfect candidate for becoming unstuck.

There's something about the process of getting stuck and then unstuck that pushes us to find purpose. It forces us to define for ourselves what we desire but have denied ourselves. Similar to how the inconvenience of road construction may force you to try a new route to work, being stuck can help you find your way. The frustration caused by being stuck will force you to answer the question "what do I want?" which is the first step in getting what you truly want. The greater your struggle is to get unstuck, the greater your sense of purpose will become.

I'm not suggesting we become irresponsible and pursue selfish desires. I'm suggesting we allow ourselves to re-engage with our God-given purpose and passions by allowing ourselves to dream a little. Be honest with yourself about what you want and why. If you aren't sure, start by completing the questions in the following activity. Don't be surprised if your answer leads you to one of these other courageous acts!

ACTIVITY: What Do I Want?

It would be amazing if _____
_____
_____
_____

What I really want is _____
_____
_____
_____

How would my life be different if I could have what I want?
_____
_____
_____

2. Release someone

Healthy relationships exist within healthy boundaries and mutually beneficial expectations, such as respect and keeping your promises. These types of expectations should be clearly communicated and agreed upon as conditions for how you relate and grow in relationships.

It is the unspoken, unrealistic, and unhealthy demands we place on others that get us stuck. The word "should" is an indication that an expectation, or a demand, is in place. We believe God should do this or shouldn't do that. Unforgiveness believes someone should or shouldn't have hurt us. Regret believes I should or shouldn't have done something.

Dealing with these types of expectations can be tricky, first because they are based on an element of truth, but also because they are usually unspoken and hide under the surface. Let's examine three areas where we may need to let go of unmet expectations in order to get unstuck.

Release God

Anger towards God for unmet expectations causes us to distance ourselves from Him. If I go through a period of several days and realize I don't have a desire to spend time in the Word or prayer, I begin to examine my heart to see if there is anger towards God. I find that it is almost always the case. My unmet expectations have caused me to distance myself from Him. As soon as I deal with what's in my heart, the desire returns.

If you walk with the Lord for any length of time, you will come to this crossroad where you must accept who He is, just as He is. I've forgiven Him for not doing what I hoped He would and had to release Him from my expectations of what I thought He should do—not because He needed it, but for my good.

My desire to be in control in my relationship with Him, which includes determining how He should or shouldn't act, keeps me from intimacy with Him. It also blinds me to His actual work in my life. Just as we want to be loved for who we really are, God wants to be loved and worshipped for who He truly is, not who we think He is or should be. He loves when we let Him be God.

I release God from this expectation: _____
_____
_____
_____

Release another person

When we release another person from an expectation or demand we've placed on them (often subconsciously and usually unsuccessfully), we give them the freedom to be who God created them to be. Entering into a relationship based only on our own expectations is actually entering a relationship with those demands, rather than with that person. The relationship is only as successful as that person's ability to read my mind, meet my unmet needs, and be who I want them to be. When they fail to do so, I feel justified in being hurt, angry, and disappointed. This is called co-dependency, and it's a primary way we can get stuck in unhealthy relationship cycles.

Forgiveness is releasing someone from an expectation they didn't meet and requiring nothing from them in exchange. We must take it a step further and release them from future expectations. Letting go of our unspoken and unhealthy expectations makes us able to see and experience people as God created them. This is the basis of true relationship and unconditional love.

I release _____ from this expectation: _____
_____
_____
_____

Release yourself

What expectations have you placed upon yourself that have you stuck in cycles of shame, perfectionism, self-hatred, and/or self-destructive behavior? Releasing yourself from your own unmet expectations can be a powerful way to get free and begin moving forward again. Rebecca found the freedom to be her true self when she let go of the unrealistic standards she had established for herself. Margot was able to change her health patterns when she let go of her regret for past failures.

Short-term regret can be beneficial for repentance and serve to shape future behaviors. But long-term regret is punishing yourself over and over again for something you did or didn't do. It prevents you from repenting and moving on because it holds you in the past. Once again, you can recognize regret by the presence of "should" in your inner dialogue. It sounds like this: "I should have done this" or "I shouldn't have done that." Regret is a lie that is based in truth (you probably should or shouldn't have done that) but is twisted to keep you ruminating and blaming yourself for the outcome. This appears to be an attack from the enemy about your past but is actually an attack on your future. It's deception trying to convince you the past prevents you from having a better future.

It's easy to get caught up in regretful thinking, wishing you had done things differently, and feeling like those opportunities may never present themselves again. We think this way because we have a finite understanding of how God works, and we think in terms of the timeline of our lives. But God, who exists outside of time, can pull things from your past, like missed opportunities, into your future so you collide with them. Those opportunities may take a different form, and those relationships may be composed of different people, but the nature of the promise He gave you will be fulfilled.

I release myself from this expectation: _____
_____
_____
_____

3. Let others be mad or disappointed in you.

Fear of man, also known as people-pleasing, is a major cause of being stuck. It can keep you from being authentic, taking risks, or saying hard things. Oddly enough, it can require courage to let someone be mad at you. Not everyone will celebrate your growth and progress—especially if they benefit from you being stuck. Don't let someone who wants to stay stuck keep you from getting unstuck. For example, when someone gets angry at you because you've implemented a healthy boundary in your life, that's a reflection of their unhealthiness. Don't let them convince you it's a reflection of yours!

I've spent years trying to convince others not to believe the lies they believe about me. I've tried to prove them wrong, often at the expense of my own authenticity and peace. I finally learned the hard way that I can't compete with their lies. Sometimes people don't want to know the truth because the truth doesn't fit their narrative, need, or dysfunction. The kindest thing you can do for that person (and for yourself) is to allow them to be mad or disappointed. It's scary to do so, especially if you don't want to lose the relationship, but it will free you up to live in truth when you aren't bound to someone else's lies.

What someone else believes about you is ultimately between them and God. Part of surrender is entrusting others, including their perceptions and opinions, into the hands of the Lord. We can trust Him with our reputations—not so much because He's worried about what people think of us, but because our identity rests securely with Him, regardless of what people think or do. You cannot have a fear of man AND be free from man.

The truth is, some people won't know what to do with the way God created you...and that's okay. Sometimes people reject you or put labels on you because they don't know how to handle what God put in you. It's easier to find fault in you than to find fault in their own thinking. When you get unstuck, not everyone will celebrate your momentum. When you begin living more fully within your purpose, some will be intimidated, and others will be jealous. Even Jesus was misunderstood and mislabeled when He lived out His purpose. When He stepped out into His ministry, He was accused of sourcing His power from Beelzebub, another name for Satan (Luke 11:14–26). If Jesus was misunderstood and rejected, you will be, too.

It's courageous to lay down our need to be liked, approved, and understood by man and entrust who we truly are to the One who created us. We place the highest value on His approval, and in turn, we are able to experience what it means to be fully loved, accepted, and celebrated for who we are.

4. Have the hard conversation

I've heard it said, "Your relationships are only as healthy as the conversations you have within them." Many relationships stay stuck, not because of things that were said, but because of the things that were left unsaid. Hard conversations require courage, and that tells me that great relationships require courage. Examples of hard conversations that will help you get unstuck may include delivering an apology, establishing a healthy boundary, or expressing vulnerability in some way. It's human nature to avoid these sorts of conversations, even though we know it's something we should do. It's not the conversation itself we are avoiding. More than anything, it is the pain it might bring. It's the risk of pain that requires courage.

One of the things that makes these conversations so intimidating is when emotions run high and we let them get the best of us. Most of the time, it has been my thinking about the conversation that has caused this, not the actual conversation. We're afraid of how the other person might respond, so we enter the conversation guarded and full of anxiety. We also avoid delivering messages that might be hurtful to the other person. We say it's because we don't want to hurt them, but what we really avoid is the guilt we feel for hurting them. Again, we're avoiding the pain the conversation might bring.

How do you know it's time for a hard conversation? I've noticed any time I start to feel either resentment towards someone or a desire to avoid someone, it is an indication that I may need to have a conversation with that person. When we shrink back from hard conversations, we resent ourselves for being inauthentic to who we are and what we believe.

Ironically, we spend a great deal of time dreading and delaying difficult conversations, and yet, we are almost always relieved when they are over. The longer you delay the conversation, the longer you delay your peace. We hope the problem will go away so we don't have to take the risk. The longer we wait, the more the misunderstandings, hurt feelings, and unmet expectations are able to develop into strongholds.

We don't have control over what the other person might do or say, but we are responsible for our contributions. Hard conversations are most beneficial when discovering truth is the goal. Remember that truth is only discovered when humility is present. When we initiate these conversations from our pride, our goal becomes being proven right. When we initiate them from a place of humility, our goal becomes discovering truth.

Here are two tips to help you prepare for a hard conversation:
1. Ask the Holy Spirit to prepare your heart, which includes rooting out your own lies before engaging the conversation.
2. Go into the conversation with the goal of learning. Sometimes the lies I believe don't get exposed until I'm in the middle of having a hard conversation with someone who is brave enough to reveal them!

5. Wrestle with the gap

It's natural to struggle with your faith when there is a gap between what you expected God to do and what you experienced. It takes courage to bring our disappointment before the Lord, but He longs to reveal Himself to you in the gap. Some of my deepest revelations of who He is have come when I've wrestled with my faith. Start by telling God what you expected and what you've experienced. Be very authentic and share your disappointment and anger. He's not afraid of either! Then get quiet before Him and invite Him to speak to you. He wants to bring healing to your disappointment, perspective to your gap, and invite you into deeper places of trust.

When a threshold is a limiter on our lives, it holds us back. But when we begin to see our threshold as an opening to something new, like the threshold of a door, it propels us forward. Ask God what He's teaching or developing in you with each threshold. Determining to grow the most you can is a surefire way to be propelled forward.

If we look at how God designed our brains, we can learn something about how He created us to live. Our minds are amazing, and scientists are only beginning to understand how they work. One thing we know for sure, our brains are lazy.

They automatically work to conserve energy and avoid cognitive dissonance. As a musician, I understand that dissonance happens when two tones clash. Cognitive dissonance occurs when there is a conflict between what I believe and what I'm experiencing. Ironically, learning occurs when cognitive dissonance occurs. It is the friction or confusion between the existing belief and the conflicting belief that forces the brain to learn. Surprisingly, confusion is an essential part of the learning process.

It is no wonder God allows us to go through seasons of confusion and struggle. What feels like abandonment and silence at the moment is our Teacher preparing us for a season of exponential and rapid growth. He's never stretching us without purpose. He always stretches us FOR our purpose. Dissonance in this season leads to a beautiful composition in the next. God is always growing us for what is to come.

We resist places of wrestling in our lives, but that's precisely where we find God. It's when we wrestle with the gap between righteousness and grace that we discover His truth. It's the gap between what we see and what He promises is true where we learn to trust. It's the tension between justice and mercy where we discover His heart. I'm convinced believers who avoid wrestling with these things end up developing weak or extreme theology and lack authentic experience with the heart of the Father. I don't know any great men or women of God who haven't had prolonged seasons of wrestling with God. This wrestling with our faith develops intimacy with Him.

FILLING THE GAP

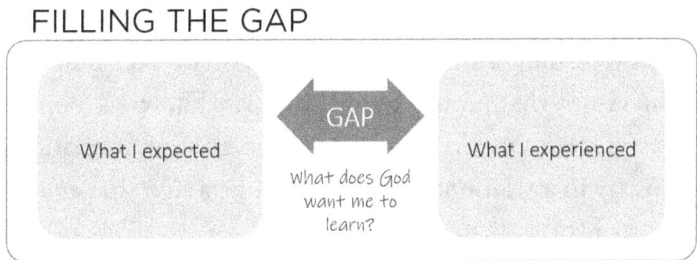

ACTIVITY: Learning in the Gap
1. I expected this to happen _____
   _____.
2. This is what happened _____
   _____.
3. I'm disappointed about this _____
   _____.
4. What do You want me to see or learn in the gap? ___
   _____.

6. Let something end

Sometimes that friendship, job, or ministry that you are fighting to keep is the very thing that needs to die so something new can form in your life. We've covered how death precedes life in the Kingdom of God, so I won't belabor this point. I just know I don't want to get to heaven and realize that I kept the wrong "things" alive and, as a result, missed out on the best things God had for me! Don't get me wrong—some things are certainly worth fighting to keep alive. But without heaven's perspective, it's hard to know which ones.

Endings are frequently part of how you get unstuck. The conclusion of something in your life is very different than running from or avoiding a situation. Jesus will never ask us to run from a situation because doing so would void our need for Him. But He very well may initiate an ending to invite you into greater trust in Him. That's a big reason you can know it's Him. If it requires greater trust in Him to walk away from a relationship than to stay in a relationship, that might be a sign that an ending is necessary and beneficial.

Endings can feel like failures. But somehow, in the Kingdom of God, they are not. Instead, they lead to new beginnings. Letting go and allowing something to end requires surrender, which is perhaps the reason we are reluctant to do so. If we could see what was on the other side, it wouldn't feel like a loss or a failure at all!

7. Challenge your version of events

If there is a situation you are stuck on, challenge your story about what happened. What assumptions may be skewing your ability to see the truth, own your part, and move on? Author and speaker Cy Wakeman says the best way to challenge your version of events is to ask yourself, "What do I know to be true?" We often equate what we *think* to be true with what we *know* to be true. The two are not the same. The facts of a situation are easily clouded by our emotions and faulty interpretations, leading us to create our own story about what has happened. When we strip away everything but the facts and focus only on what we know to be true, it empowers us to see the situation more objectively. Cy calls this editing your story. She encourages you to write out your version of events and cross out anything that isn't truth. What remains is what you know to be true.

I recently had an exchange with another leader via text message. The conversation started off very matter-of-factly, but quickly became confrontational. I know, I know…I should have just called him instead of continuing to text. That was my first mistake. Eventually, he quit texting back. I started to play out many scenarios in my mind: He was mad at me, he was telling on me, he was writing one really long mean text, etc. That was my second mistake. With each new scenario, my anxiety grew and my desire to protect myself became greater. By the time I was done imagining scenarios, the situation was blown out of proportion!

Fortunately, I recognized that my thinking had spiraled and I decided to edit my story. There were only two things I knew to be true: 1) The conversation was confrontational with many opportunities for offense. 2) He hadn't texted me back. Other than that, the rest of my thinking was speculation. Editing your story is a great way to identify lies you believe that are influencing your version of events!

Based on the truth, I decided to give him the benefit of the doubt. There could be any number of reasons he hadn't texted back, so fretting about it wasn't going to benefit the relationship. The next day, he reached out to me and we had a great conversation that only strengthened our relationship. Because I was most interested in dealing with truth, I was open, humble, and ready for that conversation.

Once we edit our story, we may find that reality looks vastly different than what we thought. Imagine if the Israelites would have challenged their version of events in regards to the giants. They might have entered Canaan 40 years earlier! Seeing your situation differently will give you the freedom to respond to truth instead of reacting to the story you've created.

Our brain naturally categorizes what happens to us. In an effort to create as much clarity and safety as possible, our brain engages in binary thinking. We may label something as either good or bad, a decision as either right or wrong, and someone as for us or against us, etc. This black-and-white thinking helps us make sense of our experiences, but at the expense of truly understanding them. As our brain sorts, it bends our interpretation of events to fit into one of the two categories. I'm sure you can easily see how this opens the door for deception.

I spoke with a mom recently who was feeling overwhelmed by her responsibilities at home. She felt she was constantly falling behind on housework. On top of this, she compared herself to her mother and mother-in-law—nearly impossible standards! Despite her many strengths as a parent, her housekeeping made her feel inadequate. If she fell short of her standard, by default she was a failure. Her binary thinking deceived her into believing she was either good or bad, and as a result, she could either be proud of herself or ashamed.

It was easy for me to see she wasn't failing or inadequate. The gap wasn't in her housekeeping but in her thinking. I encouraged her to challenge her thinking. Instead of either/or thinking, she could think in terms of a spectrum. She might be more successful at keeping the house clean some days than others but not a failure in any day. Spectrum thinking says a situation may not be good or bad, but neutral. It says one decision may be better than another, and both may be "right." And it says someone might be for us AND still act in selfish ways towards us.

It takes courage to challenge the way you see and categorize what happens to you. We see what we want to see because it agrees with our beliefs and protects us, but it also prevents us from seeing what we need to see. I don't know about you, but I want God's version of events. I don't want to think a thought, say a word, or do anything that is out of alignment with His version. But that requires me to lay aside my assumptions and exchange it for His truth.

Reflection Question: What do I know to be true about my situation?

_____
_____
_____
_____
_____

Reflection Question: In what way(s) is my binary thinking keeping me stuck?

_____
_____
_____
_____
_____

Reflection Question: Ask the Holy Spirit, "What am I not seeing that You want me to see?"

_____
_____
_____
_____
_____

8. Bless those who have hurt you

This one may seem out of place, but I assure you it's life changing when it comes to getting unstuck. One of the greatest privileges we have as believers is the choice to love our enemies, pray for those who persecute us (by definition to cause you unfair trouble), and bless those who curse us. We've been given the power to curse or to bless. When we choose to bless, especially those who don't deserve it, it causes massive shifts in the spiritual realm. This courageous act moves us from a place of victimhood to a place of freedom. It liberates us from needing anything from the person that wounded us so deeply.

To "curse" means to wish ill on someone. The enemy wants us to curse others because then it gives him legal ground to rob us of blessing and destiny. It goes against our nature because pride wants to return the favor—to repay the insult with insult, to hurt those who hurt you.

To "bless" means to speak well of and to appeal to an authority to invoke blessing. When was the last time you spoke well of an "enemy" before God? When was the last time you asked God to bless them? Here's what I've discovered: If I don't bless them, I become bitter. If I don't pray for them, I become judgmental and self-righteous. We're instructed to do these things because they are good for us!

Here are three ways you can bless those who have hurt you:

- **Thank God for them.** Get very specific and thank Him for the great qualities He gave them. In doing so, you are speaking well of them before God. You are giving them honor AND giving honor to God!
- **Ask God to bless them.** Ask God to reveal Himself to them, and pray that their needs would be met. It's impossible to pray for someone daily and not grow in Christlike love and compassion for them. Prayer is one of the tools we have for bringing truth into our situation!

- **Ask God for an opportunity to bless them.** This may not be practical or wise in every situation, but there are occasions the Lord will open the door for you to do something to bless a person who has hurt you. It seems backward to give to someone who has taken from you, but it's Biblical.

Our words can bring death or life, and we are responsible for the consequences of our words (Proverbs 18:21). There is no degree of offense or hurt that gives us a free pass to speak poorly of others, but every offense is an opportunity for us to bless others. Curses have power, but blessings have greater power. When I bless those who curse me, it not only gets me unstuck in that place of hurt, but it also aligns me to receive His blessings elsewhere in my life. We reap what we sow, and in blessing others, we reap a blessing.

Furthermore, how we handle situations when we've been wronged determines how trustworthy we are. If God can't trust us not to become offended, He won't be able to trust us with greater influence. He wants to trust us with more, but that means He must first trust us to respond His way to betrayal and offense. Can God trust you with an offense? Can He trust you to turn the other cheek? Can He trust you to bless those who have hurt you?

9. Stop defending yourself

When we are wronged, misrepresented, or slandered, everything in us rises up and wants to defend our cause. 1 Peter 2:23 says that Jesus left His case in the hands of His Father. He was made a public spectacle, and yet, He trusted His Father to be His defense attorney. This is how Jesus was able to stay silent when He was mocked and accused. This isn't to say we shouldn't have a voice or that we shouldn't be bold to speak the truth when prompted by the Holy Spirit. It is to say that we must commit our defense into His hands. This is a true measure of trust.

Our need to defend ourselves comes from fear. The lie of victimhood says no one protects me, so I must protect myself. Our desire to protect ourselves is an open door for deception because we build strongholds to do so. It's the lie of self-sufficiency. You see, He's always willing to defend us, but He won't compete with our efforts to defend ourselves. It makes me wonder how many times in my life I've missed out on His defense because I was busy defending myself. If you are still rehashing situations in your mind, this is an indication that you aren't trusting God. God wants to be your Defender in your thought-life, too!

One of the most powerful prayers of surrender you can pray is, "Father, defend me if and how You see it fit." That simple prayer shows both confidences in His ability to defend us AND His wisdom in knowing what that looks like through a redemptive lens.

If you're still not convinced you should let go of your need for defense, here are some additional reasons:

- When we trust Him to defend us, it allows Him to reveal His truth to us in the process. In other words, my need to defend myself or justify my behavior hinders His desire to transform me!
- Part of trusting God to be your defender is knowing that, over time, your character and the fruit of what God develops in you during the process will be your defense. Letting your character speak for itself may not be the fastest defense, but it's the most convincing one.
- When you defend yourself at someone else's expense, you are in sin. Let God surface truth, and be patient

while He does. Those who defend themselves the loudest and defend their character by attacking someone else's character have something to hide. They aren't defending; they are actually hiding, projecting, and manipulating.
- If you trust Him to defend you, you won't need to defend yourself at all. Jesus trusted His Father to be His defense, and God used His resurrection to bring eternal glory! In other words, all of eternity will serve as His defense!

10. Do something bold

When was the last time you would have described yourself as bold? When you were much younger? When you took a risk and changed careers? Or perhaps you've never thought of yourself that way. I can assure you, you have boldness in your DNA. Our souls love comfort, but our spirits love boldness.

I am not a big fan of creating New Year's resolutions. These tend to be ambiguous and uninspiring, so they motivate us for a bit but lose steam quickly. Instead, I create a bold list each year. I know it's just semantics, but there's something about the concept of doing "bold things" that inspires me, that stirs my spirit. There are a lot of bold things I could do in a year, but I only include things that align with who I am becoming and aspire to be in the Kingdom of God. I want to look back at the end of the year and know my boldness mattered—that it had Kingdom value.

Everything that I put on the list scares me a little; otherwise, it doesn't make the list. This is because I want to grow my trust in the Lord every single day of the year. Bold things require bold trust. I'm going to pick things that require me to rely on God and/or others, and not just my strength or abilities.

Not all bold things are automatically big things. Some items on the list are small steps towards a bigger goal. For example, I may include a hard conversation I need to have with someone with the goal of having a restored relationship. Ultimately, each goal requires me to examine the place of my commitment and make a radical decision about what I truly want. Will I remain committed to my comfort and avoid that hard conversation, or will I become more committed to that relationship and step out? Each small act has a big and eternal Kingdom impact.

ACTIVITY: Create a Bold List

If you were to make a bold list of things you want to do this year, what would make the cut? Create a bold list of no more than 10 items. If you complete them before the year is over, you can always add to them, but I find it's best to start with a manageable number and go from there.

1. _____
   _____

2. _____
   _____

3. _____
   _____

4. _____
   _____

5. _____
   _____

Chapter 10: Act with Courage

6. _____

7. _____

8. _____

9. _____

10. _____

CHAPTER 11

TRUST THE PROCESS

Once you've acted with courage, you must trust the process. Here's the thing—you can't control the process AND trust the process at the same time. If you're trying to control the process, it's the equivalent of resisting it. We want to control the process so we can control how we experience it and more importantly, so we can control the outcome. This is the formulaic thinking we discussed in Chapter 7.

To start with, trusting the process looks like making peace with the things you can't control. If you want to get unstuck, you'll have to give up a lot of control. It's a package deal. Since that's easier said than done, here are some tips to help you let go and trust the process:

Focus on your process, and let others have their own.
Since beginning to get unstuck, I've been tempted to "help" others get unstuck. After all, once you've experienced freedom,

you will want that for others, too! Remember, not everyone wants to get unstuck—even if they say they do. These are the people who start a new diet on Monday and have already blown it by Thursday. They are more committed to staying stuck than they are changing. I know because I've been one of them.

You are fully responsible for your process, but you are not responsible for anyone else's process. Sure, you may become part of their process as a confidant, encourager, or coach, but you can never own someone else's process for them. You can never cross a threshold for another person.

When I was young, one of our pet cats gave birth to a litter of kittens. I remember hovering over the momma, eagerly awaiting the arrival of each kitten. After giving birth to a couple of babies, the mom was becoming distressed, and we could see that the next kitten was breech. I hated to see her struggle, so I decided to "help" out and reached down and grabbed the portion of the kitten I could see. While I was able to get the kitten out with one swift move, the momma was not happy. She made a terrible noise and lunged at my arm with claws extended. She didn't just scratch me; she curled her claws under my skin and grabbed ahold of me. If you've ever been aggressively clawed by a cat, you understand the unreasonable amount of pain that can come from such small claws. I wouldn't wish that kind of pain on my worst enemy! I was trying to help, but she didn't want it.

To get unstuck, you have to really want to be unstuck. If you try to help someone who doesn't really want to get unstuck, you'll end up getting clawed in the process. It can be hard to sit back and watch someone spin their wheels, but you can't be more invested in someone's freedom than they are.

Chapter 11: Trust the Process

You don't have to do it perfectly. Give yourself grace.

Think progress, not perfection. If things feel messy right now, that's a good indication of progress. What is happening in you is simultaneously messy and beautiful. The two feel contradictory and exclusive of one another, but they aren't. Remember, you're changing deeply established thinking patterns and breaking long-standing cycles in your life. If this was easy to do, everyone would be better at it!

Remember that antique dresser my mom restored? Once she had stripped off the layers of paint to expose the wood grain, she sanded and applied several coats of polyurethane. For those of you who have worked with polyurethane, you know the first coat isn't all that special. In fact, after the first coat dries, you sand it down and reapply. It's a messy process, but it's the process that brings out the beauty of the wood grain and the shine of the polyurethane. If you accidentally smudge one of the layers, you can just repeat that step in the process. The process allows for imperfections while still yielding a great result. I love that God's processes work the same way; you don't have to do them perfectly to get His end result. He's built grace into the process.

Another reason it's important to give yourself grace is that it allows you to be authentic throughout. The more we pursue perfection, the more we have to pretend—and pretending actually works against the process. Authenticity embraces imperfection to get the best result. What if we gave ourselves permission to choose authenticity over perfection in the process? And in the same vein, gave others that same freedom? Trusting the process means trusting you'll get where you need to go, even if it doesn't happen the way you think it should.

Since getting unstuck is all about learning new ways of doing something, learning happens frequently in the context of mistakes. You are demolishing old strongholds and learning new ways to think about yourself, others, and God, and the enemy won't pack up and take his lies with him without first putting up a fight. Some days you are going to rock your new truth. Other days, you might catch yourself beginning to spiral. Instead of getting mad at yourself for not doing it perfectly, just reach down and "grab that coin" any time you recognize a thought out of alignment with truth. It's never too late to restart a thought process!

Take it one step at a time.

It can be overwhelming to try to cross your threshold in one swift step. Instead, take it one step, one act of courage at a time. You don't need a complete plan to move forward. Just take the first step and trust the Holy Spirit to show you the next. Many thresholds take weeks, months, or even years to cross. If you rush it, you'll likely end up repeating it. I've learned processes work best when they aren't forced. Remember how the farmer is patient for the harvest because he understands the principle of process? The more you understand the principle of process, the more patient you'll become.

Getting unstuck is like a traffic jam getting unjammed. If you've ever been stuck in traffic, you know that the flow of traffic doesn't get restored all at once. Instead, one car at the front of the line begins to move forward, allowing the car behind it to move, and so on and so forth. It's a process for traffic to resume. Every step you take is like a single car moving. It may not seem significant by itself, but the collective forward progress is substantial.

There's also no set amount of time you stay in a process before moving on. Some may be quicker than others, some you may have to repeat, and some you may stay in for a while. Part of trusting the process is trusting the timing of the process and knowing you'll get there when you get there. It's easier to be patient with the process when you focus on one step at a time.

Find the blessing in the process.

Blessings and struggles are not mutually exclusive. My friend Pastor Mark Hornback says that the blessing is found IN the struggle. My flesh feels the opposite, but my spirit knows it's true. Every Kingdom process contains a blessing. Kingdom thinking looks for and celebrates the blessing even when things are hard.

God gives us what we need in ways we wouldn't choose for ourselves. He uses imperfect situations and imperfect people to bring about His perfect purposes in your life. We often reject His methods because they don't fit our preferences, and in doing so, we resist His will. He delights in making beauty from ashes, and your current chapter of feeling stuck is only one portion of your ashes-to-beauty story.

My dad has a habit of keeping anything and everything just in case there is a slight chance it can meet a need at some point in time. You might say he is a pack rat. He sees "potential" I don't recognize. Countless times I've been doing a project and needed something and he will temporarily disappear and come back with one of his obscure treasures, perfect for the job. While I'm not condoning hoarding, I do see how my heavenly Father is even more resourceful with what I give Him than my earthly father is (which is saying something!). I'm so thankful my Savior subscribes to the belief that one man's junk is another man's treasure.

Jesus can use anything, even the state of being stuck, to bring about His purposes in your life. He can leverage that impossible situation you are facing to draw you out of passive waiting and into bold action. He can utilize that disappointing situation to invite you into a place of joy only He can provide. Your state of being stuck just might be what He needs to lead you into the next chapter of your life.

What would it look like to embrace the process instead of resisting the parts of the process that are messy, uncomfortable, hard to understand, or downright painful? Instead of spending our energy resisting, being defensive, and digging our heels in, we could spend our energy wringing out the "towel" to get the most out of it.

If things feel unfamiliar, you are making progress.

We gravitate towards what feels familiar because familiar feels safe. We make choices based on familiarity, even if it's not the best choice. We are even drawn towards familiar dysfunction, which is why many children of addicts grow up to either become or marry an addict. From this example, you can see familiar doesn't mean beneficial. Quite the opposite, it's a sign you are making progress when things feel unfamiliar.

The process of change can be costly and has some painful but temporary consequences. Even once you've passed through the threshold, it will still take time to settle into a new normal. Any time you create change in your life, there is a period of adjustment. If you change your diet or sleeping routine, your body needs to adjust. If you change how you interact with another person, it takes a while for that relationship to fall into a new normal. In the meantime, adjusting requires work. It's worth it to stay in that tension while a new norm is being established.

Chapter 11: Trust the Process

Trust that your breaking is leading to a breakthrough.

The word "threshold" originates from the word thresh and is the same word used for a threshing floor. In Old Testament times, a threshing floor was the place wheat was taken after it came out of the fields. It was the place of breaking, separating, and purifying. It's where chaff, the part that is not usable, is trampled on and broken away from the wheat kernels. The light chaff is carried away by the wind, and what remains is the usable portion of the wheat plant. God uses these threshing situations to remove the chaff from our lives.

Our decision to cross a threshold has significant ramifications in the spiritual realm. Crossing a threshold often initiates a chain reaction of things in the spiritual realm, both from heaven's vantage point and from hell's. The great news here lies in the fact that heaven always wins when we choose God. We don't need to be afraid of hell's activity, but we also must not be ignorant. Once you cross your threshold, you may experience great resistance or even betrayal from others. You may go through a season of loneliness or brokenness. You may struggle to surrender what you've left behind. All hell may break loose in your life, as the devil does everything he can to pull you back into a place of being stuck.

I believe the Holy Spirit led Jesus into a threshing floor experience. In Matthew 3, John baptizes Jesus, and the Holy Spirit descends upon Him. Once this happens, the Father speaks, "*This is my dearly loved Son, who brings Me great joy.*" This encounter is a threshold where Jesus officially steps into His ministry. But note what happens immediately following this: The Holy Spirit leads Jesus into the wilderness to fast for 40 days and be tempted by the devil. The Lord allowed the enemy to do everything he could to trample Him, beat Him down, and get Him to disobey

His Father. The enemy did everything he could to get Jesus to do something that would take away His Father's joy.

I believe Jesus not only chose obedience to the Father for those moments in the wilderness but also that He chose the cross in the wilderness. Any of the devil's temptations would have offered Jesus a way out. And yet, He opted in—for your sake and mine. The threshing floor is always an opportunity for us, in the midst of pain and testing, to opt into what God has for us. The most profound decisions you make in your life may not be just the thresholds you choose to cross, but rather the choices you make to trust Him amid the threshing.

Threshing is necessary for the wheat to fulfill a higher purpose. Without this stage in the process, the grain would be useless. If you want to be used by God, you will have threshing floor seasons of your life. God, in His infinite wisdom and love, understands that painful experiences break down our hearts so what remains is usable. When Jesus left the wilderness, His place of threshing, He left filled with the power of the Holy Spirit (Luke 4:14). What happened in the desert prepared Him for what was to come.

If you are experiencing threshing, it is because God has something bigger for you. The enemy desperately wants you to believe God is beating you up. But in reality, God is allowing your circumstances to trample out anything in you that is not of Him. It may not feel like His love at that moment, but in reality, it is His deepest love at work in your life. God's expressions of love can feel painful because He's way more interested in your freedom than He is your comfort. And just as Jesus's season of threshing was temporary, your threshing floor is temporary.

Please remember, this threshing is not your final destination. It is merely part of the process of you fulfilling a greater purpose for your life. It will be a short season compared to the extended period of blessing that is coming! After the chaff has blown away and a pile of wheat remains, that pile doesn't look very appealing or impressive—until it is gathered up for use. 1 Peter 5:10 says, *"In his kindness God called you to share in his eternal glory by means of Christ Jesus. So after you have suffered a little while, he will restore, support, and strengthen you, and he will place you on a firm foundation."* He will break you down to nothing before He builds you up to be something.

Zechariah 9:12 says, *"I promise this very day that I will repay two blessings for each of your troubles."* The Lord promises a double portion of blessings compared to the pain we've experienced. You'll look back on this season of threshing and see all the chaff shed from your life, and realize what a gift the trampling and beating was! I promise! Brokenness precedes breakthrough. A season of brokenness heralds a season of breakthrough.

The season of slander and unfair treatment I went through was a threshing floor season for me. And while it was very painful, what I gained from the experience far outweighed what it cost me. In that pain, I cried out to the Lord on my knees, asking for justice. He responded with this very clear promise to me: "Your vindication will far outlast your vilification. Your pain has been for a season, but your reward will last for many seasons." I knew then my weeping may last for a night, but joy would come in the morning.

The process of getting unstuck expands your capacity to experience what God has for you. Like carving out a pumpkin creates room, Jesus uses our times of feeling frustrated and stuck to begin to carve out the areas of our hearts that keep us from breaking through to the next season of life.

King David is an excellent example of this. Throughout the Book of Psalms, he cries out to God whenever he feels stuck (which is often!). In Psalm 69:1–4, he says, *"Save me, O God, for the floodwaters are up to my neck. Deeper and deeper I sink into the mire; I can't find a foothold. I am in deep water, and the floods overwhelm me. I am exhausted from crying for help; my throat is parched. My eyes are swollen with weeping, waiting for my God to help me. Those who hate me without cause outnumber the hairs on my head. Many enemies try to destroy me with lies, demanding that I give back what I didn't steal."*

This cry of anguish sounds like a man who is stuck in a dead end and without hope! And yet, over and over again, David experiences breakthrough in his thinking and his relationship with the Lord. He goes on to speak of experiencing God's unfailing love and faithfulness. Without the struggle of feeling stuck, David would not have experienced God's love in that place. Many of the moments when David felt most stuck were moments when he cried out that he was waiting for the Lord to move on his behalf. It was those seasons of waiting and feeling stuck that reduced David down to a man who was wholly dependent on the Lord.

In cooking, a reduction describes the process of thickening and intensifying the flavor of something by simmering or boiling. God never reduces us without reason, but He does reduce us FOR our purpose. God reduces David to prepare him for the breakthrough to come.

There's a popular saying that says, "another level, another devil." While it may be true that your opposition grows as the Lord leads you into new places, that saying emphasizes the wrong thing. A more accurate statement may be another level, another reducing. A season of decrease always precedes a season of increase. This is so we won't take the glory, but rather give the glory. James 4:10 says, *"Humble yourselves before the Lord, and he will lift you up in honor."* We resist the process that produces humility, but only because we don't truly understand how God honors humility. When God does a reducing work in us, it's always with the intent to honor us. What feels humiliating at the moment will soon reveal itself as an honor! What feels like a step backward will soon prove to be a giant step forward! That's how breakthrough works!

Be encouraged—your breakthrough is often just on the other side of the place you feel stuck. It's just past the point you want to give up and just beyond the moment you think you've exhausted your options. Think of the disciples who watched their great teacher crucified before their very eyes. His breaking was our breakthrough. Jesus's last breath on the cross evaporated their hopes of Jesus conquering the Roman Empire. Indeed, that tomb appeared to be a dead end, but we know His death was the beginning of life. What feels like a dead end to you is a starting point for Jesus. What feels like our weakness is an invitation for His strength. What feels like your breaking is the beginning of your breakthrough.

CHAPTER 12

IT'S NOT JUST ABOUT YOU

In the Old Testament, we find the story of Jacob, whose name means "cheat" and "deceiver." Jacob has a history of shady dealings. He conspires with his mom, deceives his father, and steals the family blessing from his brother, Esau. He was a con artist, a liar, and a manipulator. Despite this pattern, there is something inside of Jacob that longs to be more than a cheater.

After many years, Jacob is set to return home to face his brother for the first time since stealing his blessing. Afraid Esau will kill him when he returns, he sends his wife and children ahead along with all of his possessions and he stays behind. Add to the list that he's also a coward. In seeing his brother, he would have to face the consequences of what he had done to him. But I wonder if what scared him most was admitting who he was—a cheater. He was face-to-face with the reality of who he was, and he didn't like what he saw. He was stuck.

There's something in Jacob that wants greatness, just as there is something in each of us that calls us to be bigger, better. And like us, I don't think Jacob knew how to find that purpose. His cheating, self-sufficient ways hadn't gotten him as far as he expected or hoped. His self-sufficiency left him wanting more. Jacob is exhausted, afraid, alone, and without his family or possessions. For the first time in his life, he can't control the situation or manipulate the outcome.

At this point, he is visited by an angel of the Lord. It's just like the Lord to show up when we are at the end of our rope! What happens next is pivotal. Jacob demands the angel give him a blessing and begins to wrestle with him. It sounds strange, right? It's not that different than how we might initiate a conflict with someone when we are feeling powerless. I think Jacob did this out of desperation to gain a sense of control.

They wrestled throughout the night until daybreak, at which point the angel delivers a blow to Jacob's hip that gave him a limp for the rest of his life. It was then that Jacob realized what had happened. Genesis 32:30 says, *"I have seen God face-to-face, yet my life has been spared."* At the end of the struggle, Jacob gets God's blessing and his life begins to change.

If you follow the trajectory of his life after this encounter, you will learn that he faces his failures and sins. He confronts the lies he's believed and repents for his self-sufficiency. He restores relationship with Esau and takes responsibility for his behavior. He crosses his threshold.

His transformation is made official when God gives him a new name, Israel, and tells Jacob he is going to establish great nations from him. Israel means "prince." Think about this: He went from having a name that meant cheat to a name that meant prince. From a name of dishonor to a name of honor. He went from being defined by his past to being defined by God's purpose for him.

It's the remarkable story of how God brings freedom and redemption to a man who is stuck. Even more than that, it's a story of how one man getting unstuck altered the course of history. Jacob's lineage includes Levi, Moses, David, and Jesus. Getting unstuck not only changed the trajectory of his life, but of God's people. It wasn't just a Jacob thing, it was a generational thing. A destiny thing.

Here's my point: Getting unstuck is bigger and more important than you can see. Your freedom has a ripple effect. Your friends will see the change and look at their own lives in a new way. The people you influence (and we all have influence) will find you more trustworthy. If you are a parent, the things you choose to ignore will get passed on, but every step you make toward God and toward healing has an impact on future generations. Do you remember my friends who were fixing up their old house to fix what was rotten? They've fixed it for themselves, but the outcome is that future generations will benefit from their hard work. When you live in your destiny, you not only get free yourself, but you open doors for others to follow you. It's worth the work. Trust me.

ACKNOWLEDGEMENTS

I want to thank my family and friends for all of your support while writing this book. I'm grateful for your feedback when I needed to bounce ideas off of you, your encouragement when I was feeling I bit off more than I could chew, and even your distractions when my brain needed a break. You're the same group of people who encouraged and guided me on my own journey to get unstuck, so each one of you are part of the story represented in these pages. I want to specifically thank my mom for all of her help in editing this book, as well as those who gave me permission to use your personal "unstuck stories" to illustrate my points. I'm incredibly blessed.

www.ingramcontent.com/pod-product-compliance
Lightning Source LLC
Chambersburg PA
CBHW072152100526
44589CB00015B/2200